HISTORY OF

KING CHARLES II

OF ENGLAND

HISTORY OF
KING CHARLES II
OF ENGLAND

JACOB ABBOTT

Serenity
Publishers, LLC
ROCKVILLE, MARYLAND
2009

ISBN: 978-1-60450-681-5

Published by Serenity Publishers
An Arc Manor Company
P. O. Box 10339
Rockville, MD 20849-0339
www.SerenityPublishers.com

Printed in the United States of America/United Kingdom

CONTENTS

PREFACE

The author of this series has made it his special object to confine himself very strictly, even in the most minute details which he records, to historic truth. The narratives are not tales founded upon history, but history itself, without any embellishment or any deviations from the strict truth, so far as it can now be discovered by an attentive examination of the annals written at the time when the events themselves occurred. In writing the narratives, the author has endeavored to avail himself of the best sources of information which this country affords; and though, of course, there must be in these volumes, as in all historical accounts, more or less of imperfection and error, there is no intentional embellishment. Nothing is stated, not even the most minute and apparently imaginary details, without what was deemed good historical authority. The readers, therefore, may rely upon the record as the truth, and nothing but the truth, so far as an honest purpose and a careful examination have been effectual in ascertaining it.

I

INFANCY

KING CHARLES the Second was the son and successor of King Charles the First. These two are the only kings of the name of Charles that have appeared, thus far, in the line of English sovereigns. Nor is it very probable that there will soon be another. The reigns of both these monarchs were stained and tarnished with many vices and crimes, and darkened by national disasters of every kind, and the name is thus connected with so many painful associations in the minds of men, that it seems to have been dropped, by common consent, in all branches of the royal family.

The reign of Charles the First, as will be seen by the history of his life in this series, was characterized by a long and obstinate contest between the king and the people, which brought on, at last, a civil war, in which the king was defeated and taken prisoner, and in the end beheaded on a block, before one of his own palaces. During the last stages of this terrible contest, and before Charles way himself taken prisoner, he was, as it were, a fugitive and an outlaw in his own dominions. His wife and family were scattered in various foreign lands, his cities and castles were in the hands of his enemies, and his oldest son, the prince Charles, was the object of special hostility. The prince incurred, therefore, a great many dangers, and suffered many heavy calamities in his early years. He lived to see these calamities pass away, and, after they were gone, he enjoyed, so far as his own personal safety and welfare were concerned, a tranquil and prosperous life. The storm, however, of trial and suffering which enveloped the evening of his father's days, darkened the morning of his own. The life of Charles the First was a river rising gently, from quiet springs, in a scene of verdure and sunshine, and flowing gradually into rugged and gloomy regions, where at last it falls into a terrific abyss, enveloped in darkness and storms. That of Charles the Second, on the other hand, rising in the wild and rugged mountains where the parent stream was engulfed, commences its course by leaping frightfully from precipice to precipice, with turbid and foaming waters, but emerges at last into a smooth and smiling land, and flows through it prosperously to the sea.

Prince Charles's mother, the wife of Charles the First, was a French princess. Her name was Henrietta Maria. She was unaccomplished, beautiful, and very spirited woman. She was a Catholic, and the English people, who were very decided in their hostility to the Catholic faith, were extremely jealous of her. They watched all her movements with the utmost suspicion. They were very unwilling that an heir to the crown should arise in her family. The animosity which they felt against her husband the king, which was becoming every day more and more bitter, seemed to be doubly inveterate and intense toward her. They published pamphlets, in which they called her a daughter of Heth, a Canaanite, and an idolatress, and expressed hopes that from such a worse than pagan stock no progeny should ever spring.

Henrietta was at this time—1630—twenty-one years of age, and had been married about four years. She had had one son, who had died a few days after his birth. Of course, she did not lead a very happy life in England. Her husband the king, like the majority of the English people, was a Protestant, and the difference was a far more important circumstance in those days than it would be now; though even now a difference in religious faith, on points *which either party deems essential,* is, in married life, an obstacle to domestic happiness, which comes to no termination, and admits of no cure. If it were possible for reason and reflection to control the impetuous impulses of youthful hearts, such differences of religious faith would be regarded, where they exist, as an insurmountable objection to a matrimonial union.

The queen, made thus unhappy by religious dissensions with her husband, and by the public odium of which she was the object, lived in considerable retirement and seclusion at St. James's Palace, in Westminster, which is the western part of London. Here her second son, the subject of this history, was born, in May, 1630, which was ten years after the landing of the pilgrims on the Plymouth rock. The babe was very far from being pretty, though he grew up at last to be quite a handsome man. King Charles was very much pleased at the birth of his son. He rode into London the next morning at the head of a long train of guards and noble attendants, to the great cathedral church of St. Paul's, to render thanks publicly to God for the birth of his child and the safety of the queen. While this procession was going through the streets, all London being out to gaze upon it, the attention of the vast crowd was attracted to the appearance of a star glimmering faintly in the sky at midday. This is an occurrence not very uncommon, though it seldom, perhaps, occurs when it has so many observers to witness it. The star was doubtless Venus, which, in certain circumstances, is often bright enough to be seen when the sun is above the horizon. The populace of London, however, who were not in those days very profound astronomers, regarded the shining of the star as a supernatural occurrence altogether, and as portending the future greatness and glory of the prince whose natal day it thus unexpectedly adorned.

Preparations were made for the baptism of the young prince in July. The baptism of a prince is an important affair, and there was one circumstance which gave a peculiar interest to that of the infant Charles. The Reformation had not been long established in England, and this happened to be the first occasion on which an heir to the English crown had been baptized since the Liturgy of the English Church had been arranged. There is a chapel connected with the palace of St. James, as is usual with royal palaces in Europe, and even, in fact, with the private castles and mansions of the higher nobility. The baptism took place there. On such occasions it is usual for certain persons to appear as sponsors, as they are called, who undertake to answer for the safe and careful instruction of the child in the principles of the Christian faith. This is, of course, mainly a form, the real function of the sponsors being confined, as it would appear, to making magnificent presents to their young godchild, in acknowledgment of the distinguished honor conferred upon them by their designation to the office which they hold. The sponsors, on this occasion, were certain royal personages in France, the relatives of the queen. They could not appear personally, and so they appointed proxies from among the higher nobility of England, who appeared at the baptism in their stead, and made the presents to the child. One of these proxies was a duchess, whose gift was a jewel valued at a sum in English money equal to thirty thousand dollars.

The oldest son of a king of England receives the title of Prince of Wales; and there was an ancient custom of the realm, that an infant prince of Wales should be under the care, in his earliest years, of a Welsh nurse, so that the first words which he should learn to speak might be the vernacular language of his principality. Such a nurse was provided for Charles. Rockers for his cradle were appointed, and many other officers of his household, all the arrangements being made in a very magnificent and sumptuous manner. It is the custom in England to pay fees to the servants by which a lady or gentleman is attended, even when a guest in private dwellings; and some idea may be formed of the scale on which the pageantry of this occasion was conducted, from the fact that one of the lady sponsors who rode to the palace in the queen's carriage, which was sent for her on this occasion, paid a sum equal to fifty dollars each to six running footmen who attended the carriage, and a hundred dollars to the coachman; while a number of knights who came on horseback and in armor to attend upon the carriage, as it moved to the palace, received each a gratuity of two hundred and fifty dollars. The state dresses on the occasion of this baptism were very costly and splendid, being of white satin trimmed with crimson.

The little prince was thus an object of great attention at the very commencement of his days, His mother had his portrait painted, and sent it to *her* mother in France. She did not, however, in the letters which accompanied the picture, though his mother, praise the beauty of her child. She said, in fact, that he was so ugly that she was ashamed of him, though his size and plumpness, she added, atoned for the want of beauty. And then he was so comically serious and grave in the expression of his countenance! the queen said she verily believed that he was wiser than herself.

As the young prince advanced in years, the religious and political difficulties in the English nation increased, and by the time that he had arrived at an age when he could begin to receive impressions from the conversation and intercourse of those around him, the Parliament began to be very jealous of the influence which his mother might exert. They were extremely anxious that he should be educated a Protestant, and were very much afraid that his mother would contrive to initiate him secretly into the ideas and practices of the Catholic faith.

She insisted that she did not attempt to do this, and perhaps she did not; but in those days it was often considered right to make false pretensions and to deceive, so far as this was necessary to promote the cause of true religion. The queen did certainly make some efforts to instill Catholic principles into the minds of some of her children; for she had other children after the birth of Charles. She gave a daughter a crucifix one day, which is a little image of Christ upon the cross, made usually of ivory, or silver, or gold, and also a rosary, which is a string of beads, by means of which the Catholics are assisted to count their prayers. Henrietta gave these things to her daughter secretly, and told her to hide them in her pocket, and taught her how to use them. The Parliament considered such attempts to influence the minds of the royal children as very heinous sins, and they made such arrangements for secluding the young prince Charles from his mother, and putting the others under the guidance of Protestant teachers and governors, as very much interfered with Henrietta's desires to enjoy the society of her children. Since England was a Protestant realm, a Catholic lady, in marrying an English king, ought not to have expected, perhaps, to have been allowed to bring up her children in her own faith; still, it must have been very hard for a mother to be forbidden to teach her own children what she undoubtedly believed was the only possible means of securing for them the favor and protection of Heaven.

There is in London a vast storehouse of books, manuscripts, relics, curiosities, pictures, and other memorials of by-gone days, called the British Museum. Among the old records here preserved are various letters written by Henrietta, and one or two by Charles, the young prince, during his childhood. Here is one, for instance, written by Henrietta to her child, when the little prince was but eight years of age, chiding him for not being willing to take his medicine. He was at that time under the charge of Lord Newcastle.

"CHARLES,
I am sorry that I must begin my first letter with chiding you, because I hear that you will not take phisicke, I hope it was onlie for this day, and that to-morrow you will do it for if you will not,

13

I must come to you, and *make* you take it, for it is for your health. I have given order to mi Lord of Newcastle to send mi word to-night whether you will or not. Therefore I hope you will not give me the paines to goe; and so I rest, your affectionate mother,

HENRIETTE MARIE."

The letter was addressed

"*To* MI DEARE SONNE *the Prince.*"

The queen must have taken special pains with this her first letter to her son, for, with all its faults of orthography, it is very much more correct than most of the epistles which she attempted to write in English. She was very imperfectly acquainted with the English language, using, as she almost always did, in her domestic intercourse, her own native tongue.

Time passed on, and the difficulties and contests between King Charles and his people and Parliament became more and more exciting and alarming. One after another of the king's most devoted and faithful ministers was arrested, tried, condemned, and beheaded, notwithstanding all the efforts which their sovereign master could make to save them. Parties were formed, and party spirit ran very high. Tumults were continually breaking out about the palaces, which threatened the personal safety of the king and queen. Henrietta herself was a special object of the hatred which these outbreaks expressed. The king himself was half distracted by the overwhelming difficulties of his position. Bad as it was in England, it was still worse in Scotland. There was an actual rebellion there, and the urgency of the danger in that quarter was so great that Charles concluded to go there, leaving the poor queen at home to take care of herself and her little ones as well as she could, with the few remaining means of protection yet left at her disposal.

There was an ancient mansion, called Oatlands, not very far from London, where the queen generally resided during the absence of her husband. It was a lonely place, on low and level ground, and surrounded by moats filled with water, over which those who wished to enter passed by draw bridges. Henrietta chose this place for her residence because she thought she should be safer there from mobs and violence. She kept the children all there except the Prince of Wales, who was not allowed to be wholly under her care. He, however, often visited his mother, and she sometimes visited him.

During the absence of her husband, Queen Henrietta was subjected to many severe and heavy trials. Her communications with him were often interrupted and broken. She felt a very warm interest in the prosperity and success of his expedition, and sometimes the tidings she received from him encouraged her to hope that all might yet be well. Here, for instance, is a note which she addressed one day to an officer who had sent her a letter from the king, that had come enclosed to him. It is written in a broken English, which shows how imperfectly the foreign lady had learned the language of her adopted country. They who understand the French language will be interested in observing that most of the errors which the writer falls into are those which result naturally from the usages of her mother tongue.

Queen Henrietta to Sir Edward Nicholas.

"MAISTRE NICHOLAS,
I have reseaved your letter, and that you send me from the king, which writes me word he as been vere well reseaved in Scotland; that both the armi and the people have shewed a creat joy to see the king, and such that theay say was never seen before. Pray God it may continue.

Your Friend,
HENRIETTE MARIE R."

At one time during the king's absence in Scotland the Parliament threatened to take the queen's children all away from her, for fear, as they said, that she would make papists of them. This danger alarmed and distressed the queen exceedingly. She declared that she did not intend or desire to bring up her children in the Catholic faith. She knew this was contrary to the wish of the king her husband, as well as of the people of England. In order to diminish the danger that the children would be taken away, she left Oatlands herself, and went to reside at other palaces, only going occasionally to visit her children. Though she was thus absent from them in person, her heart was with them all the time, and she was watching with great solicitude and anxiety for any indications of a design on the part of her enemies to come and take them away.

At last she received intelligence that an armed force was ordered to assemble one night in the vicinity of Oatlands to seize her children, under the pretext that the queen was herself forming plans for removing them out of the country and taking them to France. Henrietta was a lady of great spirit and energy, and this threatened danger to her children aroused all her powers. She sent immediately to all the friends about her on whom she could rely, and asked them to come, armed and equipped, and with as many followers as they could muster, to the park at Oatlands that night. There were also then in and near London a number of officers of the army, absent from their posts on furlough. She sent similar orders to these. All obeyed the summons with eager alacrity. The queen mustered and armed her own household, too, down to the lowest servants of the kitchen. By these means quite a little army was collected in the park at Oatlands, the separate parties coming in, one after another, in the evening and night. This guard patrolled the grounds till morning, the queen herself animating them by her presence and energy. The children, whom the excited mother was thus guarding, like a lioness defending her young, were all the time within the mansion, awaiting in infantile terror some dreadful calamity, they scarcely knew what, which all this excitement seemed to portend.

The names and ages of the queen's children at this time were as follows:

Charles, prince of Wales, the subject of this story, eleven.

Mary, ten. Young as she was, she was already married, having been espoused a short time before to William, prince of Orange, who was one year older than herself.

James, duke of York, seven. He became afterward King James II.

Elizabeth, six.

Henry, an infant only a few months old.

The night passed away without any attack, though a considerable force assembled in the vicinity, which was, however, soon after disbanded. The queen's fears were, nevertheless, not allayed. She began to make arrangements for escaping from the kingdom in ease it should become necessary to do so. She sent a certain faithful friend and servant to Portsmouth with orders to get some vessels ready, so that she could fly there with her children and embark at a moment's notice, if these dangers and alarms should continue.

She did not, however, have occasion to avail herself of these preparations. Affairs seemed to take a more favorable turn. The king came back from Scotland. He was received by his people, on his arrival, with apparent cordiality and good will. The queen was, of course, rejoiced to welcome him home, and she felt relieved and protected by his presence. The city of London, which had been the main seat of disaffection and hostility to the royal family, began to show symptoms of returning loyalty and friendly regard. In reciprocation for this, the king determined on making a grand entry into the city, to pay a sort of visit to the authorities. He rode, on this occasion, in a splendid chariot of state, with the little prince by his side. Queen Henrietta came next, in an open carriage of her own, and the other children, with other carriages, followed in the train. A long cortege of guards and attendants, richly dressed and magnificently mounted, preceded and followed the royal family, while the streets were lined with thousands of spectators, who waved handkerchiefs and banners, and shouted God save the king! In the midst of this scene of excitement and triumph, Henrietta rode quietly along, her anxieties relieved, her sorrows and trials ended, and her heart bounding with happiness and hope. She was once more, as she conceived, reunited to her husband and her children, and reconciled to the people of her realm. She thought her troubles were over Alas! they had, on the contrary, scarcely begun.

II

PRINCE CHARLES'S MOTHER

THE indications and promises of returning peace and happiness which gave Prince Charles's mother so much animation and hope after the return of her husband from Scotland were all very superficial and fallacious. The real grounds of the quarrel between the king and his Parliament, and of the feelings of alienation and ill will cherished toward the queen, were all, unfortunately, as deep and extensive as ever; and the storm, which lulled treacherously for a little time, broke forth soon afterward anew, with a frightful violence which it was evident that nothing could withstand. This new onset of disaster and calamity was produced in such a way that Henrietta had to reproach herself with being the cause of its coming.

She had often represented to the king that, in her opinion, one main cause of the difficulties he had suffered was that he did not act efficiently and decidedly, and like a man, in putting down the opposition manifested against him on the part of his subjects; and now, soon after his return from Scotland, on some new spirit of disaffection showing itself in Parliament, she urged him to act at once energetically and promptly against it. She proposed to him to take an armed force with him, and proceed boldly to the halls where the Parliament was assembled, and arrest the leaders of the party who were opposed to him. There were five of them who were specially prominent. The queen believed that if these five men were seized and imprisoned in the Tower, the rest would be intimidated and overawed, and the monarch's lost authority and power would be restored again.

The king was persuaded, partly by the dictates of his own judgment, and partly by the urgency of the queen, to make the attempt. The circumstances of this case, so far as the action of the king was concerned in them, are fully related in the history of Charles the First. Here we have only to speak of the queen, who was left in a state of great suspense and anxiety in her palace at Whitehall while her husband was gone on his dangerous mission.

The plan of the king to make this irruption into the great legislative assembly of the nation had been kept, so they supposed, a very profound secret, lest the members whom he was going to arrest should receive warning of their danger and fly. When the time arrived, the king bade Henrietta farewell, saying that she might wait there an hour, and if she received no ill news from him during that time, she might be sure that he had been successful, and that he was once more master of his kingdom. The queen remained in the apartment where the king had left her, looking continually at the watch which she held before her, and counting the minutes impatiently as the hands moved slowly on. She had with her one confidential friend, the Lady Carlisle, who sat with her and seemed to share her solicitude, though she had not been entrusted with the secret. The time passed on. No ill tidings came; and at length the hour fully expired, and Henrietta, able to contain herself no longer, exclaimed with exultation, "Rejoice with me; the hour is gone. From this time my husband is master of his realm. His enemies in Parliament are all arrested before this time, and his kingdom is henceforth his own."

It certainly is possible for kings and queens to have faithful friends, but there are so many motives and inducements to falsehood and treachery in court, that it is *not* possible, generally, for them to distinguish false friends from true. The Lady Carlisle was a confederate with some of the very men whom Charles had gone to arrest. On receiving this intimation of their danger, she sent immediately to the houses of Parliament, which were very near at hand, and the obnoxious members received warning in time to fly. The hour had indeed elapsed, but the king had met with several unexpected delays, both in his preparations for going, and on his way to the House of Commons, so that when at last he entered, the members were gone. His attempt, however, unsuccessful as it was, evoked a general storm of indignation and anger, producing thus all the exasperation which was to have been expected from the measure, without in any degree accomplishing its end. The poor queen was overwhelmed with confusion and dismay when she learned the result. She had urged her husband forward to an extremely dangerous and desperate measure, and then by her thoughtless indiscretion had completely defeated the end. A universal and utterly uncontrollable excitement burst like a clap of thunder upon the country as this outrage, as they termed it, of the king became known, and the queen was utterly appalled at the extent and magnitude of the mischief she had done.

The mischief was irremediable. The spirit of resentment and indignation which the king's action had aroused, expressed itself in such tumultuous and riotous proceedings as to render the continuance of the royal family in London no longer safe. They accordingly removed up the river to Hampton Court, a famous palace on the Thames, not many miles from the city. There they remained but a very short time. The dangers which beset them were evidently increasing. It was manifest that the king must either give up what he deemed the just rights and prerogatives of the crown, or prepare to maintain them by war. The queen urged him to choose the latter alternative. To raise the means for doing this, she proposed that she should herself leave the country, taking with her, her jewels, and such other articles of great value as could be easily carried away, and by means of them and her personal exertions, raise funds and forces to aid her husband in the approaching struggle.

The king yielded to the necessity which seemed to compel the adoption of this plan. He accordingly set off to accompany Henrietta to the shore. She took with her the young Princess Mary; in fact, the ostensible object of her journey was to convey her to her young husband, the Prince of Orange, in Holland. In such infantile marriages as theirs, it is not customary, though the marriage ceremony be performed, for the wedded pair to live together till they arrive at years a little more mature.

The queen was to embark at Dover. Dover was in those days the great port of egress from England to the Continent. There was, and is still, a great castle on the cliffs to guard the harbor and the town. These cliffs are picturesque and high, falling off abruptly in chalky precipices to the sea. Among them at one place is a sort of dell, by which there is a gradual descent to the water. King Charles stood upon the shore when Henrietta sailed away, watching the ship as it receded from his view, with tears in his eyes. With all the faults, characteristic of her nation, which Henrietta possessed, she was now his best and truest friend, and when she was gone he felt that he was left desolate and alone in the midst of the appalling dangers by which he was environed. The king went back to Hampton Court. Parliament sent him a request that he would come and reside nearer to the capital, and enjoined upon him particularly not to remove the young Prince of Wales. In the mean time they began to gather together their forces, and to provide munitions of war. The king did the same. He sent the young prince to the western part of the kingdom, and retired himself to the northward, to the city of York, which he made his head-quarters. In a word, both parties prepared for war.

In the mean time, Queen Henrietta was very successful in her attempts to obtain aid for her husband in Holland. Her misfortunes awakened pity, with which, through her beauty, and the graces of her conversation and address, there was mingled a feeling analogous to love. Then, besides, there was something in her spirit of earnest and courageous devotion to her husband in the hours of his calamity that won for her a strong degree of admiration and respect.

There are no efforts which are so efficient and powerful in the accomplishment of their end as those which a faithful wife makes to rescue and save her husband. The heart, generally so timid, seems to be inspired on such occasions with a preternatural courage, and the arm, at other times so feeble and helpless, is nerved with unexpected strength. Every one is ready to second and help such efforts, and she who makes them is surprised at her success, and wonders at the extent and efficiency of the powers which she finds herself so unexpectedly able to wield.

The queen interested all classes in Holland in her plans, and by her personal credit, and the security of her diamonds and rubies, she borrowed large sums of money from the government, from the banks, and from private merchants. The sums which she thus raised amounted to two millions of pounds sterling, equal to nearly ten millions of dollars. While these negotiations were going on she remained in Holland, with her little daughter, the bride, under her care, whose education she was carrying forward all the time with the help of suitable masters; for, though married, Mary was yet a child. The little husband was going on at the same time with his studies too.

Henrietta remained in Holland a year. She expended a part of her money in purchasing military stores and supplies for her husband, and then set sail with them, and with the money not expended, to join the king. The voyage was a very extraordinary one. A great gale of wind began to blow from the northeast soon after the ships left the port, which increased in violence for nine days, until at length the sea was lashed to such a state of fury that the company lost all hope of ever reaching the land. The queen had with her a large train of attendants, both ladies and gentlemen; and there were also in her suit a number of Catholic priests, who always accompanied her as the chaplains and confessors of her household. These persons had all been extremely sick, and had been tied into their beds on account of the excessive rolling of the ship, and their own exhaustion and helplessness. The danger increased, until at last it became so extremely imminent that all the self-possession of the passengers was entirely gone. In such protracted storms, the surges of the sea strike the ship with terrific force, and vast volumes of water fall heavily upon the decks, threatening instant destruction—the ship plunging awfully after the shock, as if sinking to rise no more. At such moments, the noble ladies who accompanied the queen on this voyage would be overwhelmed with terror, and they filled the cabins with their shrieks of dismay. All this time the queen herself was quiet and composed. She told the ladies not to fear, for "queens of England were never drowned."

At one time, when the storm was at its height, the whole party were entirely overwhelmed with consternation and terror. Two of the ships were engulfed and lost. The queen's company thought that their own was sinking. They came crowding into the cabin where the priests were lying, sick and helpless, and began all together to confess their sins to them, in the Catholic mode, eager in these their last moments, as they supposed, to relieve their consciences in any way from the burdens of guilt which oppressed them. The queen herself did not participate in these fears. She ridiculed the absurd confessions, and rebuked the senseless panic to which the terrified penitents were yielding; and whenever any mitigation of the violence of the gale made it possible to do any thing to divert the minds of her company, she tried to make amusement out of the odd and strange dilemmas in which they were continually placed, and the ludicrous disasters and accidents which were always befalling her servants and officers of state, in their attempts to continue the etiquette and ceremony proper in attendance upon a queen, and from which even the violence of such a storm, and the imminence of such danger, could not excuse them. After a fortnight of danger, terror, and distress, the ships that remained of the little squadron succeeded in getting back to the port from which they had sailed.

The queen, however, did not despair. After a few days of rest and refreshment she set sail again, though it was now in the dead of winter. The result of this second attempt was a prosperous voyage, and the little fleet arrived in due time at Burlington, on the English coast, where the queen landed her money and her stores. She had, however, after all, a very narrow escape, for she was very closely pursued on her voyage by an English squadron. They came into port the night after she had landed, and the next morning she was awakened by the crashing of cannon balls and the bursting of bomb shells in the houses around her, and found, on hastily rising, that the village was under a bombardment from the ships of her enemies. She hurried on some sort of dress, and sallied forth with her attendants to escape into the fields. This incident is related fully in the history of her husband, Charles the First; but there is one circumstance, not there detailed, which illustrates very strikingly that strange combination of mental greatness and energy worthy of a queen, with a simplicity of affections and tastes which we should scarcely expect in a child, that marked Henrietta's character. She had a small dog. Its name was Mike. They say it was an ugly little animal, too, in all eyes but her own. This dog accompanied her on the voyage, and landed with her on the English shore. On the morning, however, when she fled from her bed to escape from the balls and bomb shells of the English ships, she recollected, after getting a short distance from the house, that Mike was left behind. She immediately returned, ran up to her chamber again, seized Mike, who was sleeping unconsciously upon her bed, and bore the little pet away from the scene of ruin which the balls and bursting shells were making, all astonished, no doubt, at so hurried and violent an abduction. The party gained the open fields, and seeking shelter in a dry trench, which ran along the margin of a field, they crouched there together till the commander of the ships was tired of firing.

The queen's destination was York, the great and ancient capital of the north of England York was the head quarters of King Charles's army, though he himself was not there at this time. As soon as news of the queen's arrival reached York, the general in command there sent down to the coast a detachment of two thousand men to escort the heroine, and the stores and money which she had brought, to her husband's capital. At the head of this force she marched in triumph across the country, with a long train of ordnance and baggage wagons loaded with supplies. There were six pieces of cannon, and two hundred and fifty wagons loaded with the money which she had obtained in Holland. The whole country was excited with enthusiasm at the spectacle. The enthusiasm was increased by the air and bearing of the queen, who, proud and happy at this successful result of all her dangers and toils, rode on horseback at the head of her army like a general, spoke frankly to the soldiers, sought no shelter from the sun and rain, and ate her meals, like the rest of the army, in a bivouac in the open field. She had been the means, in some degree, of leading the king into his difficulties, by the too vigorous measures she had urged him to take in the case of the attempted parliamentary arrest. She seems to have been determined to make that spirit of resolution and energy in her, which caused the mischief then, atone for it by its efficient usefulness now. She stopped on her march to summon and *take* a town, which had been hitherto in the hands of her husband's enemies, adding thus the glory of a conquest to the other triumphs of the day.

In fact, the queen's heart was filled with pride and pleasure at this conclusion of her enterprise, as is very manifest from the frequent letters which she wrote to her husband at the time. The king's cause revived. They gradually approached each other in the operations which they severally conducted, until at last the king, after a great and successful battle, set off at the head of a large escort to come and meet his wife. They met in the vale of Keynton, near Edgehill, which is on the southern borders of Warwickshire, near the center of the island. The meeting was, of course, one of the greatest excitement and pleasure. Charles praised the high courage and faithful affection of his devoted wife, and she was filled with happiness in enjoying the love and gratitude of her husband.

The pressure of outward misfortune and calamity has always the same strong tendency as was manifest in this case to invigorate anew all the ties of conjugal and domestic affection, and thus to create the happiness which it seems to the world to destroy. In the early part of Charles and Henrietta's married life, while every thing external went smoothly and prosperously with them, they were very far from being happy. They destroyed each other's peace by petty disputes and jars about things of little consequence, in which they each had scarcely any interest except a desire to carry the point and triumph over the other. King Charles himself preserved a record of one of these disputes. The queen had received, at the time of her marriage, certain estates, consisting of houses and lands, the income of which was to be at her disposal, and she wished to appoint certain treasurers to take charge of this property. She had made out a list of these officers in consultation with her mother. She gave this list to Charles one night, after he was himself in bed. He said he would look at it in the morning, but that she must remember that, by the marriage treaty, *he* was to appoint those officers. She said, in reply, that a part of those whom she had named were English. The king said that he would look at the paper in the morning, and such of the English names as he approved he would confirm, but that he could not appoint any Frenchmen. The queen answered that she and her mother had selected the men whom she had named, and she would not have any body else. Charles rejoined that the business was not either in her power or her mother's, and if she relied on such an influence to effect her wishes, he would not appoint *any body* that she recommended. The queen was very much hurt at this, and began to be angry. She said that if she could not put in whom she chose, to have the care of her property, she would not have any such property. He might take back her houses and lands, and allow her what he pleased in money in its stead. Charles replied by telling her to remember whom she was speaking to; that he could not be treated in that manner; and then the queen, giving way to lamentations and tears, said she was wretched and miserable; every thing that she wanted was denied her, and whatever she recommended was refused on the very account of her recommendation. Charles tried to speak, but she would not hear; she went on with her lamentations and complaints, interrupted only by her own sobs of passion and grief.

The reader may perhaps imagine that this must have been an extreme and unusual instance of dissension between this royal pair; but it was not. Cases of far greater excitement and violence sometimes occurred. The French servants and attendants, whom the queen very naturally preferred, and upon whom the king was as naturally inclined to look with suspicion and ill will, were a continual source of disagreement between them. At last, one afternoon, the king, happening to come into that part of the palace at Whitehall where the queen's apartments were situated, and which was called "the queen's side", found there a number of her gentlemen and lady attendants in a great frolic, capering and dancing in a way which the gay Frenchmen probably considered nothing extraordinary, but which King Charles regarded as very irreverent and unsuitable conduct to be witnessed in the presence of an English queen. He was very much displeased. He advanced to Henrietta, took her by the arm, conducted her sternly to his own side of the palace, brought her into one of his own apartments, and locked the door. He then sent an officer to direct all the French servants and attendants in the queen's apartments to leave the palace immediately, and repair to Somerset House, which was not far distant, and remain there till they received further orders. The officer executed these commands in a very rough manner. The French women shrieked and cried, and filled the court yard of the palace with their clamor; but the officer paid no regard to this noise. He turned them all out of the apartments, and locked the doors after them.

The queen was rendered quite frantic with vexation and rage at these proceedings. She flew to the windows to see and to bid farewell to her friends, and to offer them expressions of her sympathy. The king pulled her away, telling her to be quiet and submit, for he was determined that they should go. The queen was determined that she would not submit. She attempted to open the windows; the king held them down. Excited now to a perfect frenzy in the struggle, she began to break out the panes with her fist, while Charles exerted all his force to restrain and confine her, by grasping her wrists and endeavoring to force her away. What a contrast between the low and sordid selfishness and jealousy evinced in such dissensions as these, and the lofty and heroic devotedness and fidelity which this wife afterward evinced for her husband in the harassing cares the stormy voyages, and the martial exposures and fatigues which she endured for his sake! And yet, notwithstanding this great apparent contrast, and the wide difference in the estimation which mankind form of the conduct of the actor in these different scenes, still we can see that it is, after all, the impulse of the same lofty and indomitable spirit which acted in both. The soul itself of the queen was not altered, nor even the character of her action. The change was in the object and aim. In the one case she was contending against the authority of a husband, to gain petty and useless victories in domestic strife; in the other, the same spirit and energy were expended in encountering the storms and tempests of outward adversity to sustain her husband and protect her children. Thus the change was a change of circumstances rather than of character.

The change was, however, none the less important on that account in its influence on the king. It restored to him the affection and sympathy of his wife, and filled his heart with inward happiness. It was a joyous change to him, though it was produced by sufferings and sorrows; for it was the very pressure of outward calamity that made his wife his friend again, and restored his domestic peace. In how many thousand instances is the same effect produced in a still more striking manner, though on a less conspicuous stage, than in the case of this royal pair! And how many thousands of outwardly prosperous families there are, from which domestic peace and happiness are gone, and nothing but the pressure from without of affliction or calamity can ever restore them!

In consequence, in a great measure, of Henrietta's efficient help, the king's affairs greatly improved, and, for a time, it seemed as if he would gain an ultimate and final victory over his enemies, and recover his lost dominion. He advanced to Oxford, and made his head quarters there, and commenced the preparations for once more getting possession of the palaces and fortresses of London. He called together a Parliament at Oxford; some members came, and were regularly organized in the two houses of Lords and Commons, while the rest remained at London and continued their sittings there. Thus there were two governments, two Parliaments, and two capitals in England, and the whole realm was rent and distracted by the respective claims of these contending powers over the allegiance of the subjects and the government of the realm.

III

QUEEN HENRIETTA'S FLIGHT

THE brightening of the prospects in King Charles's affairs which was produced, for a time, by the queen's vigorous and energetic action, proved to be only a temporary gleam after all. The clouds and darkness soon returned again, and brooded over his horizon more gloomily than ever. The Parliament raised and organized new and more powerful armies. The great Republican general, Oliver Cromwell, who afterward became so celebrated as the Protector in the time of the Commonwealth, came into the field, and was very successful in all his military plans. Other Republican generals appeared in all parts of the kingdom, and fought with great determination and great success, driving the armies of the king before them wherever they moved, and reducing town after town, and castle after castle, until it began to appear evident that the whole kingdom would soon fall into their hands.

In the mean time, the family of the queen were very much separated from each other, the children having been left in various places, exposed each to different privations and dangers. Two or three of them were in London in the hands of their father's enemies. Mary, the young bride of the Prince of Orange, was in Holland. Prince Charles, the oldest son, who was now about fourteen years of age, was at the head of one of his father's armies in the west of England. Of course, such a boy could not be expected to accomplish any thing as a general, or even to exercise any real military command. He, however, had his place at the head of a considerable force, and though there were generals with him to conduct all the operations, and to direct the soldiery, they were nominally the lieutenants of the prince, and acted, in all cases, in their young commander's name. Their great duty was, however, after all, to take care of their charge; and the army which accompanied Charles was thus rather an escort and a guard, to secure his safety, than a force from which any aid was to be expected in the recovery of the kingdom.

The queen did every thing in her power to sustain the sinking fortunes of her husband, but in vain. At length, in June, 1644, she found herself unable to continue any longer such warlike and masculine exposures and toils. It became necessary for her to seek some place of retreat, where she could enjoy, for a time at least, the quiet and repose now essential to the preservation of her life. Oxford was no longer a place of safety. The Parliament had ordered her impeachment on account of her having brought in arms and munitions of war from foreign lands, to disturb, as they said, the peace of the kingdom. The Parliamentary armies were advancing toward Oxford, and she was threatened with being shut up and besieged there. She accordingly left Oxford, and went down to the sea-coast to Exeter, a strongly fortified place, on a hill surrounded in part by other hills, and very near the sea. There was a palace within the walls, where the queen thought she could enjoy, for a time at least, the needed seclusion and repose. The king accompanied her for a few miles on her journey, to a place called Abingdon, which is in the neighborhood of Oxford, and there the unhappy pair bade each other farewell, with much grief and many tears. They never met again.

Henrietta continued her sorrowful journey alone. She reached the sea-coast in the south-western part of England, where Exeter is situated, and shut herself up in the place of her retreat. She was in a state of great destitution, for Charles's circumstances were now so reduced that he could afford her very little aid. She sent across the Channel to her friends in France, asking them to help her. They sent immediately the supplies that she needed—articles of clothing, a considerable sum of money, and a nurse. She retained the clothing and the nurse, and a little of the money; the rest she sent to Charles. She was, however, now herself tolerably provided for in her new home, and here, a few weeks afterward, her sixth child was born. It was a daughter.

The queen's long continued exertions and exposures had seriously impaired her health, and she lay, feeble and low, in her sick chamber for about ten days, when she learned to her dismay that one of the Parliamentary generals was advancing at the head of his army to attack the town which she had made her refuge. This general's name was Essex. The queen sent a messenger out to meet Essex, asking him to allow her to withdraw from the town before he should invest it with his armies. She said that she was very weak and feeble, and unable to endure the privations and alarms which the inhabitants of a besieged town have necessarily to bear; and she asked his permission, therefore, to retire to Bristol, till her health should be restored. Essex replied that he could not give her permission to retire from Exeter; that, in fact, the object of his coming there was to escort her to London, to bring her before Parliament, to answer to the charge of treason.

The queen perceived immediately that nothing but the most prompt and resolute action could enable her to escape the impending danger. She had but little bodily strength remaining, but that little was stimulated and renewed by the mental resolution and energy which, as is usual in temperaments like hers, burned all the brighter in proportion to the urgency of the danger which called it into action. She rose from her sick bed, and began to concert measures for making her escape. She confided her plan to three trusty friends, one gentleman, one lady, and her confessor, who, as her spiritual teacher and guide, was her constant companion. She disguised herself and these her attendants, and succeeded in getting through the gates of Exeter without attracting any observation. This was before Essex arrived. She found, however, before she went far, that the van of the army was approaching, and she had to seek refuge in a hut till her enemies had passed. She concealed herself among some straw, her attendants seeking such other hiding places as were at hand. It was two days before the bodies of soldiery had all passed so as to make it safe for the queen to come out of her retreat. The hut would seem to have been uninhabited, as the accounts state that she remained all this time without food, though this seems to be an almost incredible degree of privation and exposure for an English queen. At any rate, she remained during all this time in a state of great mental anxiety and alarm, for there were parties of soldiery constantly going by, with a tumult and noise which kept her in continual terror. Their harsh and dissonant voices, heard sometimes in angry quarrels and sometimes in mirth, were always frightful. In fact, for a helpless woman in a situation like that of the queen, the mood of reckless and brutal mirth in such savages was perhaps more to be dreaded than that of their anger.

At one time the queen overheard a party of these soldiers talking about *her*. They knew that to get possession of the papist queen was the object of their expedition. They spoke of getting her head and carrying it to London, saying that Parliament had offered a reward of fifty thousand crowns for it, and expressed the savage pleasure which it would give them to secure this prize, by imprecations and oaths.

They did not, however, discover their intended victim. After the whole army passed, the queen ventured cautiously forth from her retreat; the little party got together again, and, still retaining their disguises, moved on over the road by which the soldiers had come, and which was in the shocking condition that a road and a country always exhibit where an army has been marching. Faint and exhausted with sickness, abstinence, and the effects of long continued anxiety and fear, the queen had scarcely strength to go on. She persevered, however, and at length found a second refuge in a cabin in a wood. She was going to Plymouth, which is forty or fifty miles from Exeter, to the south-west, and is the great port and naval station of the English, in that quarter of the island.

She stopped at this cabin for a little time to rest, and to wait for some other friends and members of her household from the palace in Exeter to join her. Those friends were to wait until they found that the queen succeeded in making her escape, and then they were to follow, each in a different way, and all assuming such disguises as would most effectually help to conceal them. There was one of the party whom it must have been somewhat difficult to disguise. It was a dwarf, named Geoffrey Hudson, who had been a long time in the service of Henrietta as a personal attendant and messenger. It was the fancy of queens and princesses in those days to have such personages in their train. The oddity of the idea pleased them, and the smaller the dimensions of such a servitor, the greater was his value. In modern times all this is changed. Tall footmen now, in the families of the great, receive salaries in proportion to the number of inches in their stature, and the dwarfs go to the museums, to be exhibited, for a price, to the common wonder of mankind.

The manner in which Sir Geoffrey Hudson was introduced into the service of the queen was as odd as his figure. It was just after she was married, and when she was about eighteen years old. She had two dwarfs then already, a gentleman and a lady, or, as they termed it then, a *cavalier* and a *dame*, and, to carry out the whimsical idea, she had arranged a match between these two, and had them married. Now there was in her court at that time a wild and thoughtless nobleman, a great friend and constant companion of her husband Charles the First, named Buckingham. An account of his various exploits is given in our history of Charles the First. Buckingham happened to hear of this Geoffrey Hudson, who was then a boy of seven or eight years of age, living with his parents somewhere in the interior of England. He sent for him, and had him brought secretly to his house, and made an arrangement to have him enter the service of the queen, without, however, saying any thing of his design to her. He then invited the queen and her husband to visit him at his palace; and when the time for luncheon arrived, one day, he conducted the party into the dining saloon to partake of some refreshment. There was upon the table, among other viands, what appeared to be a large venison pie. The company gathered around the table, and a servant proceeded to cut the pie, and on his breaking and raising a piece of the crust, out stepped the young dwarf upon the table, splendidly dressed and armed, and, advancing toward the queen, he kneeled before her, and begged to be received into her train. Her majesty was very much pleased with the addition itself thus made to her household, as well as diverted by the odd manner in which her new attendant was introduced into her service.

The youthful dwarf was then only eighteen inches high, and he continued so until he was thirty years of age, when, to every body's surprise, he began to grow. He grew quite rapidly, and, for a time, there was a prospect that he would be entirely spoiled, as his whole value had consisted thus far in his littleness. He attained the height of three feet and a half, and there the mysterious principle of organic expansion, the most mysterious and inexplicable, perhaps, that is exhibited in all the phenomena of life, seemed to be finally exhausted, and, though he lived to be nearly seventy years of age, he grew no more.

Notwithstanding the bodily infirmity, whatever it may have been, which prevented his growth, the dwarf possessed a considerable degree of mental capacity and courage. He did not bear, however, very good-naturedly, the jests and gibes of which he was the continual object, from the unfeeling courtiers, who often took pleasure in teasing him and in getting him into all sorts of absurd and ridiculous situations. At last his patience was entirely exhausted, and he challenged one of his tormentors, whose name was Crofts, to a duel. Crofts accepted the challenge, and, being determined to persevere in his fun to the end, appeared on the battle ground armed only with a squirt. This raised a laugh, of course, but it did not tend much to cool the injured Lilliputian's anger. He sternly insisted on another meeting, and with real weapons. Crofts had expected to have turned off the whole affair in a joke, but he found this could not be done; and public opinion among the courtiers around him compelled him finally to accept the challenge in earnest. The parties met on horseback, to put them more nearly on an equality. They fought with pistols. Crofts was killed upon the spot.

After this Hudson was treated with more respect. He was entrusted by the queen with many commissions, and sometimes business was committed to him which required no little capacity, judgment, and courage. He was now, at the time of the queen's escape from Exeter, of his full stature, but as this was only three and a half feet, he encountered great danger in attempting to find his way out of the city and through the advancing columns of the army to rejoin the queen. He persevered, however, and reached her safely at last in the cabin in the wood. The babe, not yet two weeks old, was necessarily left behind. She was left in charge of Lady Morton, whom the queen appointed her governess. Lady Morton was young and beautiful. She was possessed of great strength and energy of character, and she devoted herself with her whole soul to preserving the life and securing the safety of her little charge.

The queen and her party had to traverse a wild and desolate forest, many miles in extent, on the way to Plymouth. The name of it was Dartmoor Forest. Lonely as it was, however, the party was safer in it than in the open and inhabited country, which was all disturbed and in commotion, as every country necessarily is in time of civil war. As the queen drew near to Plymouth, she found that, for some reason, it would not be safe to enter that town, and so the whole party went on, continuing their journey farther to the westward still.

Now there is one important sea-port to the westward of Plymouth which is called Falmouth, and near it, on a high promontory jutting into the sea, is a large and strong castle, called Pendennis Castle. This castle was, at the time of the queen's escape, in the hands of the king's friends, and she determined, accordingly, to seek refuge there. The whole party arrived here safely on the 29th of June. They were all completely worn out and exhausted by the fatigues, privations, and exposures of their terrible journey.

The queen had determined to make her escape as soon as possible to France. She could no longer be of any service to the king in England; her resources were exhausted, and her personal health was so feeble that she must have been a burden to his cause, and not a help, if she had remained. There was a ship from Holland in the harbor. The Prince of Orange, it will be recollected, who had married the queen's oldest daughter, was a prince of Holland, and this vessel was under his direction. Some writers say it was sent to Falmouth by him to be ready for his mother-in-law, in case she should wish to make her escape from England. Others speak of it as being there accidentally at this time. However this may be, it was immediately placed at Queen Henrietta's disposal, and she determined to embark in it on the following morning. She knew very well that, as soon as Essex should have heard of her escape, parties would be scouring the country in all directions in pursuit of her, and that, although the castle where she had found a temporary refuge was strong, it was not best to incur the risk of being shut up and besieged in it.

She accordingly embarked, with all her company, on board the Dutch ship on the very morning after her arrival, and immediately put to sea. They made all sail for the coast of France, intending to land at Dieppe. Dieppe is almost precisely east of Falmouth, two or three hundred miles from it, up the English Channel. As it is on the other side of the Channel, it would lie to the south of Falmouth, were it not that both the French and English coasts trend here to the northward.

Some time before they arrived at their port, they perceived some ships in the offing that seemed to be pursuing them. They endeavored to escape, but their pursuers gained rapidly upon them, and at length fired a gun as a signal for the queen's vessel to stop. The ball came bounding over the water toward them, but did no harm. Of course there was a scene of universal commotion and panic on board the queen's ship. Some wanted to fire back upon the pursuers, some wished to stop and surrender, and others shrieked and cried, and were overwhelmed with uncontrollable emotions of terror. In the midst of this dreadful scene of confusion, the queen, as was usual with her in such emergencies, retained all her self-possession, and though weak and helpless before, felt a fresh strength and energy now, which the imminence itself of the danger seemed to inspire. She was excited, it is true, as well as the rest, but it was, in her case, the excitement of courage and resolution, and not of senseless terror and despair. She ascended to the deck; she took the direct command of the ship; she gave instructions to the pilot how to steer; and, though there was a storm coming on, she ordered every sail to be set, that the ship might be driven as rapidly as possible through the water. She forbade the captain to fire back upon their pursuers, fearing that such firing would occasion delay; and she gave distinct and positive orders to the captain, that so soon as it should appear that all hope of escape was gone, and that they must inevitably fall into the hands of their enemies, he was to set fire to the magazine of gunpowder, in order that they might all be destroyed by the explosion.

In the mean time all the ships, pursuers and pursued, were rapidly nearing the French coast. The fugitives were hoping to reach their port. They were also hoping every moment to see some friendly French ships appear in sight to rescue them. To balance this double hope, there was a double fear. There were their pursuers behind them, whose shots were continually booming over the water, threatening them with destruction, and there was a storm arising which, with the great press of sail that they were carrying, brought with it a danger, perhaps, more imminent still.

It happened that these hopes and fears were all realized, and nearly at the same time. A shot struck the ship, producing a great shock, and throwing all on board into terrible consternation. It damaged the rigging, bringing down the rent sails and broken cordage to the deck, and thus stopped the vessel's way. At the same moment some French vessels came in sight, and, as soon as they understood the case, bore down full sail to rescue the disabled vessel. The pursuers, changing suddenly their pursuit to flight, altered their course and moved slowly away. The storm, however, increased, and, preventing them from making the harbor of Dieppe, drove them along the shore, threatening every moment to dash them upon the rocks and breakers. At length the queen's vessel succeeded in getting into a rocky cove, where they were sheltered from the winds and waves, and found a chance to land. The queen ordered out the boat, and was set ashore with her attendants on the rocks. She climbed over them, wet as they were with the dashing spray, and slippery with sea weed. The little party, drenched with the rain, and exhausted and forlorn, wandered along the shore till they came to a little village of fishermen's huts. The queen went into the first wretched cabin which offered itself, and lay down upon the straw in the corner for rest and sleep.

The tidings immediately spread all over the region that the Queen of England had landed on the coast, and produced, of course, universal excitement. The gentry in the neighborhood flocked down the next morning, in their carriages, to offer Henrietta their aid. They supplied her wants, invited her to their houses, and offered her their equipages to take her wherever she should decide to go. What she wanted was seclusion and rest. They accordingly conveyed her, at her request, to the Baths of Bourbon, where she remained some time, until, in fact, her health and strength were in some measure restored. Great personages of state were sent to her here from Paris, with money and all other necessary supplies, and in due time she was escorted in state to the city, and established in great magnificence and splendor in the Louvre, which was then one of the principal palaces of the capital.

Notwithstanding the outward change which was thus made in the circumstances of the exiled queen, she was very unhappy. As the excitement of her danger and her efforts to escape it passed away, her spirits sunk, her beauty faded, and her countenance assumed the wan and haggard expression of despair. She mourned over the ruin of her husband's hopes, and her separation from him and from her children, with perpetual tears. She called to mind continually the image of the little babe, not yet three weeks old, whom she had left so defenseless in the very midst of her enemies. She longed to get some tidings of the child, and reproached herself sometimes for having thus, as it were, abandoned her.

The localities which were the scenes of these events have been made very famous by them, and traditional tales of Queen Henrietta's residence in Exeter, and of her romantic escape from it, have been handed down there, from generation to generation, to the present day. They caused her portrait to be painted too, and hung it up in the city hall of Exeter as a memorial of their royal visitor. The palace where the little infant was born has long since passed away, but the portrait hangs in the Guildhall still.

IV

ESCAPE OF THE CHILDREN

WE left the mother of Prince Charles, at the close of the last chapter, in the palace of the Louvre in Paris. Though all her wants were now supplied, and though she lived in royal state in a magnificent palace on the banks of the Seine, still she was disconsolate and unhappy. She had, indeed, succeeded in effecting her own escape from the terrible dangers which had threatened her family in England, but she had left her husband and children behind, and she could not really enjoy herself the shelter which she had found from the storm, as long as those whom she so ardently loved were still out, exposed to all its fury. She had six children. Prince Charles, the oldest, was in the western part of England, in camp, acting nominally as the commander of an army, and fighting for his father's throne. He was now fourteen years of age. Next to him was Mary, the wife of the Prince of Orange, who was safe in Holland. She was one year younger than Charles. James, the third child, whose title was now Duke of York, was about ten. He had been left in Oxford when that city was surrendered, and had been taken captive there by the Republican army. The general in command sent him to London a prisoner. It was hard for such a child to be a captive, but then there was one solace in his lot. By being sent to London he rejoined his little sister Elizabeth and his brother Henry, who had remained there all the time. Henry was three years old and Elizabeth was six. These children, being too young, as was supposed, to attempt an escape, were not very closely confined. They were entrusted to the charge of some of the nobility, and lived in one of the

38

London palaces. James was a very thoughtful and considerate boy, and had been enough with his father in his campaigns to understand something of the terrible dangers with which the family were surrounded. The other children were too young to know or care about them, and played blindman's buff and hide and go seek in the great saloons of the palace with as much infantile glee as if their father and mother were as safe and happy as ever.

Though they felt thus no uneasiness and anxiety for themselves, their exiled mother mourned for them, and was oppressed by the most foreboding fears for their personal safety. She thought, however, still more frequently of the babe, and felt a still greater solicitude for her, left as she had been, at so exceedingly tender an age, in a situation of the most extreme and imminent danger. She felt somewhat guilty in having yielded her reluctant consent, for political reasons, to have her other children educated in what she believed a false system of religious faith, and she now prayed earnestly to God to spare the life of this her last and dearest child, and vowed in her anguish that, if the babe were ever restored to her, she would break through all restrictions, and bring her up a true believer. This vow she afterward earnestly fulfilled.

The child, it will be recollected, was left, when Henrietta escaped from Exeter, in the care of the Countess of Morton, a young and beautiful, and also a very intelligent and energetic lady. The child had a visit from its father soon after its mother left it. King Charles, as soon as he heard that Essex was advancing to besiege Exeter, where he knew that the queen had sought refuge, and was, of course, exposed to fall into his power, hastened with an army to her rescue. He arrived in time to prevent Essex from getting possession of the place. He, in fact, drove the besieger away from the town, and entered it himself in triumph. The queen was gone, but he found the child.

The king gazed upon the little stranger with a mixture of joy and sorrow. He caused it to be baptized, and named it Henrietta Anne. The name Henrietta was from the mother; Anne was the name of Henrietta's sister-in-law in Paris, who had been very kind to her in all her troubles. The king made ample arrangements for supplying Lady Morton with money out of the revenues of the town of Exeter, and, thinking that the child would be as safe in Exeter as any where, left her there, and went away to resume again his desperate conflicts with his political foes.

Lady Morton remained for some time at Exeter, but the king's cause every where declined. His armies were conquered, his towns were taken, and he was compelled at last to give himself up a prisoner. Exeter, as well as all the other strongholds in the kingdom, fell into the hands of the parliamentary armies. They sent Lady Morton and the little Henrietta to London, and soon afterward provided them with a home in the mansion at Oatlands, where the queen herself and her other children had lived before. It was a quiet and safe retreat, but Lady Morton was very little satisfied with the plan of remaining there. She wished very much to get the babe back to its mother again in Paris. She heard, at length, of rumors that a plan was forming by the Parliament to take the child out of her charge, and she then resolved to attempt an escape at all hazards.

Henrietta Anne was now two years old, and was beginning to talk a little. When asked what was her name, they had taught her to attempt to reply *princess*, though she did not succeed in uttering more than the first letters of the word, her answer being, in fact, *prah*. Lady Morton conceived the idea of making her escape across the country in the disguise of a beggar woman, changing, at the same time, the princess into a boy. She was herself very tall, and graceful, and beautiful, and it was hard for her to make herself look old and ugly. She, however, made a hump for her back out of a bundle of linen, and stooped in her gait to counterfeit age. She dressed herself in soiled and ragged clothes, disfigured her face by reversing the contrivances with which ladies in very fashionable life are said sometimes to produce artificial youth and beauty, and with the child in a bundle on her back, and a staff in her hand, she watched for a favorable opportunity to escape stealthily from the palace, in the forlorn hope of walking in that way undetected to Dover, a march of fifty miles, through a country filled with enemies.

Little Henrietta was to be a boy, and as people on the way might ask the child its name, Lady Morton was obliged to select one for her which would fit, in some degree, her usual reply to such a question. She chose the name Pierre, which sounds, at least, as much like *prah* as princess does. The poor child, though not old enough to speak distinctly, was still old enough to talk a great deal. She was very indignant at the vile dress which she was compelled to wear, and at being called a beggar boy. She persisted in telling every body whom she met that she was not a boy, nor a beggar, nor Pierre, but the *princess* saying it all, however, very fortunately, in such an unintelligible way, that it only alarmed Lady Morton, without, however, attracting the attention of those who heard it, or giving them any information.

Contrary to every reasonable expectation, Lady Morton succeeded in her wild and romantic attempt. She reached Dover in safety. She made arrangements for crossing in the packet boat, which then, as now, plied from Dover to Calais. She landed at length safely on the French coast, where she threw off her disguise, resumed her natural grace and beauty, made known her true name and character, and traveled in ease and safety to Paris. The excitement and the intoxicating joy which Henrietta experienced when she got her darling child once more in her arms, can be imagined, perhaps, even by the most sedate American mother; but the wild and frantic violence of her expressions of it, none but those who are conversant with the French character and French manners can know.

It was not very far from the time of little Henrietta's escape from her father's enemies in London, though, in fact, before it, that Prince Charles made his escape from the island too. His father, finding that his cause was becoming desperate, gave orders to those who had charge of his son to retreat to the southwestern coast of the island, and if the Republican armies should press hard upon him there, he was to make his escape, if necessary, by sea.

The southwestern part of England is a long, mountainous promontory, constituting the county of Cornwall. It is a wild and secluded region, and the range which forms it seems to extend for twenty or thirty miles under the sea, where it rises again to the surface, forming a little group of islands, more wild and rugged even than the land. These are the Scilly Isles. They lie secluded and solitary, and are known chiefly to mankind through the ships that seek shelter among them in storms. Prince Charles retreated from post to post through Cornwall, the danger becoming more and more imminent every day, till at last it became necessary to fly from the country altogether. He embarked on board a vessel, and went first to the Scilly Isles.

From Scilly he sailed eastward toward the coast of France. He landed first at the island of Jersey, which, though it is very near the French coast, and is inhabited by a French population, is under the English government. Here the prince met with a very cordial reception, as the authorities were strongly attached to his father's cause. Jersey is a beautiful isle and, far enough south to enjoy a genial climate, where flowers bloom and fruits ripen in the warm sunbeams, which are here no longer intercepted by the driving mists and rains which sweep almost perceptibly along the hill sides and fields of England.

Prince Charles did not, however, remain long in Jersey. His destination was Paris. He passed, therefore, across to the main land, and traveled to the capital. He was received with great honors at his mother's new home, in the palace of the Louvre, as a royal prince, and heir apparent to the British crown. He was now sixteen. The adventures which he met with on his arrival will be the subject of the next chapter.

James, the Duke of York, remained still in London. He continued there for two years, during which time his father's affairs went totally to ruin. The unfortunate king, after his armies were all defeated, and his cause was finally given up by his friends, and he had surrendered himself a prisoner to his enemies, was taken from castle to castle, every where strongly guarded and very closely confined. At length, worn down with privations and sufferings, and despairing of all hope of relief, he was taken to London to be tried for his life. James, in the mean time, with his brother, the little Duke of Gloucester, and his sister Elizabeth, were kept in St. James's Palace, as has already been stated, under the care of an officer to whom they had been given in charge.

The queen was particularly anxious to have James make his escape. He was older than the others, and in case of the death of Charles, would be, of course, the next heir to the crown. He did, in fact, live till after the close of his brother's reign, and succeeded him, under the title of James the Second. His being thus in the direct line of succession made his father and mother very desirous of effecting his rescue, while the Parliament were strongly desirous, for the same reason, of keeping him safely. His governor received, therefore, a special charge to take the most effectual precautions to prevent his escape, and, for this purpose, not to allow of his having any communication whatever with his parents or his absent friends. The governor took all necessary measures to prevent such intercourse, and, as an additional precaution, made James *promise* that he would not receive any letter from any person unless it came through him.

James's mother, however, not knowing these circumstances, wrote a letter to him, and sent it by a trusty messenger, directing him to watch for some opportunity to deliver it unobserved. Now there is a certain game of ball, called *tennis*, which was formerly a favorite amusement in England and on the Continent of Europe, and which, in fact, continues to be played there still. It requires an oblong enclosure, surrounded by high walls, against which the balls rebound. Such an enclosure is called a tennis court. It was customary to build such tennis courts in most of the royal palaces. There was one at St. James's Palace, where the young James, it seems, used sometimes to play.[1] Strangers had the opportunity of seeing the young prince in his coming and going to and from this place of amusement, and the queen's messenger determined to offer him the letter there. He accordingly tendered it to him stealthily, as he was passing, saying, "Take this; it is from your mother."

James drew back, replying, "I can not take it. I have promised that I will not."

The messenger reported to the queen that he offered the letter to James, and that he refused to receive it. His mother was very much displeased, and wondered what such a strange refusal could mean.

Although James thus failed to receive his communication, he was allowed at length, once or twice, to have an interview with his father, and in these interviews the king recommended to him to make his escape, if he could, and to join his mother in France. James determined to obey this injunction, and immediately set to work to plan his escape. He was fifteen years of age, and, of course, old enough to exercise some little invention.

He was accustomed, as we have already stated, to join the younger children in games of hide and go seek. He began now to search for the most recondite hiding places, where he could not be found, and when he had concealed himself in such a place, he would remain there for a very long time, until his playmates had given up the search in despair. Then, at length, after having been missing for half an hour, he would reappear of his own accord. He thought

---

[1]   It was to such a tennis court at Versailles that the great National Assembly of France adjourned when the king excluded them from their hall, at the commencement of the great Revolution, and where they took the famous oath not to separate till they had established a constitution, which has been so celebrated in history as the Oath of the Tennis Court.

that by this plan he should get the children and the attendants accustomed to his being for a long time out of sight, so that, when at length he should finally disappear, their attention would not be seriously attracted to the circumstance until he should have had time to get well set out upon his journey.

He had, like his mother, a little dog, but, unlike her, he was not so strongly attached to it as to be willing to endanger his life to avoid a separation. When the time arrived, therefore, to set out on his secret journey, he locked the dog up in his room, to prevent its following him, and thus increasing the probability of his being recognized and brought back. He then engaged his brother and sister and his other playmates in the palace in a game of hide and go seek. He went off ostensibly to hide, but, instead of doing so, he stole out of the palace gates in company with a friend named Banfield, and a footman. It was in the rear of the palace that he made his exit, at a sort of postern gate, which opened upon an extensive park. After crossing the park, the party hurried on through London, and then directed their course down the River Thames toward Gravesend, a port near the mouth of the river, where they intended to embark for Holland. They had taken the precaution to disguise themselves. James wore a wig, which, changing the color and appearance of his hair, seemed to give a totally new expression to his face. He substituted other clothes, too, for those which he was usually accustomed to wear. The whole party succeeded thus in traversing the country without detection. They reached Gravesend, embarked on board a vessel there, and sailed to Holland, where James joined the Prince of Orange and his sister, and sent word to his mother that he had arrived there in safety.

His little brother and sister were left behind. They were too young to fly themselves, and too old to be conveyed away, as little Henrietta had been, in the arms of another. They had, however, the mournful satisfaction of seeing their father just before his execution, and of bidding him a last farewell. The king, when he was condemned to die, begged to be allowed to see these children. They were brought to visit him in the chamber where he was confined. His parting interview with them, and the messages of affection and farewell which he sent to their brothers and sisters, and to their mother, constitute one of the most affecting scenes which the telescope of history brings to our view, in that long and distant vista of the past, which it enables us so fully to explore. The little Gloucester was too young to understand the sorrows of the hour, but Elizabeth felt them in all their intensity. She was twelve years old. When brought to her father, she burst into tears, and wept long and bitterly. Her little brother, sympathizing in his sister's sorrow, though not comprehending its cause, wept bitterly too. Elizabeth was thoughtful enough to write an account of what took place at this most solemn farewell as soon as it was over. Her account is as follows:

"What the king said to me on the 29th of January, 1648, the last time I had the happiness to see him.

"He told me that he was glad I was come, for, though he had not time to say much, yet somewhat he wished to say to me, which he could not to another, and he had feared 'the cruelty' was too great to permit his writing. 'But, darling,' he added, 'thou wilt forget what I tell thee.' Then, shedding an abundance of tears, I told him that I would write down all he said to me. 'He wished me,' he said, 'not to grieve and torment myself for him, for it was a glorious death he should die, it being for the laws and religion of the land.' He told me what books to read against popery. He said 'that he had forgiven all his enemies, and he hoped God would forgive them also;' and he commanded us, and all the rest of my brothers and sisters, to forgive them too. Above all, he bade me tell my mother 'that his thoughts had never strayed from her, and that his love for her would be the same to the last;' withal, he commanded me (and my brother) to love her and be obedient to her. He desired me 'not to grieve for him, for he should die a martyr, and that he doubted not but God would restore the throne to his son, and that then we should be all happier than we could possibly have been if he had lived.'

"Then taking my brother Gloucester on his knee, he said, 'Dear boy, now will they cut off thy father's head.' Upon which the child looked very steadfastly upon him. 'Heed, my child, what I say; they will cut off my head, and perhaps make thee a king; but, mark what I say! You must not be a king as long as your brothers Charles and James live; therefore, I charge you, do not be made a king by them.' At which the child, sighing deeply, replied, 'I will be torn in pieces first.' And these words, coining so unexpectedly from so young a child, rejoiced my father exceedingly. And his majesty spoke to him of the welfare of his soul, and to keep his religion, commanding him to fear God, and he would provide for him; all which the young child earnestly promised to do."

After the king's death the Parliament kept these children in custody for some time, and at last they became somewhat perplexed to know what to do with them. It was even proposed, when Cromwell's Republican government had become fully established, to bind them out apprentices, to learn some useful trade. This plan was, however, not carried into effect. They were held as prisoners, and sent at last to Carisbrooke Castle, where their father had been confined. Little Henry, too young to understand his sorrows, grew in strength and stature, like any other boy; but Elizabeth pined and sunk under the burden of her woes. She mourned incessantly her father's cruel death, her mother's and her brother's exile, and her own wearisome and hopeless captivity. "Little Harry", as she called him, and a Bible, which her father gave her in his last interview with her, were her only companions. She lingered along for two years after her father's death, until at length the hectic flush, the signal of approaching dissolution, appeared upon her cheek, and an unnatural brilliancy brightened in her eyes. They sent her father's physician to see if he could save her. His prescriptions did no good. One day the attendants came into her apartment and found her sitting in her chair, with her cheek resting upon the Bible which she had been reading, and which she had placed for a sort of pillow on the table, to rest her weary head upon when her reading was done. She was motionless. They would have thought her asleep, but her eyes were not closed. She was dead. The poor child's sorrows and sufferings were ended forever.

The stern Republicans who now held dominion over England, men of iron as they were, could not but be touched with the unhappy fate of this their beautiful and innocent victim; and they so far relented from the severity of the policy which they had pursued toward the ill-fated family as to send the little Gloucester, after his sister's death, home to his mother.

V

THE PRINCE'S RECEPTION AT PARIS

So complicated a story as that of the family of Charles can not be related, in all its parts, in the exact order of time; and having now shown under what circumstances the various members of the family made their escape from the dangers which threatened them in England, we return to follow the adventures of Prince Charles during his residence on the Continent, and, more particularly in this chapter, to describe his reception by the royal family of France. He was one of the first of the children that escaped, having arrived in France in 1646. His father was not beheaded until two years afterward.

In order that the reader may understand distinctly the situation in which Charles found himself on his arrival at Paris, we must first describe the condition of the royal family of France at this time. They resided sometimes at Fontainebleau, a splendid palace in the midst of a magnificent park about forty miles from the city. Henrietta, it will be recollected, was the sister of a king of France. This king was Louis XIII. He died, however, not far from the time of Queen Henrietta's arrival in the country, leaving his little son Louis, then five years old, heir to the crown. The little Louis of course became king immediately, in name, as Louis XIV., and in the later periods of his life he attained to so high a degree of prosperity and power, that he has been, ever since his day, considered one of the most renowned of all the French kings. He was, of course, Prince Charles's cousin. At the period of Prince Charles's arrival, however, he was a mere child, being then about eight years old. Of course, he was too young really to exercise any of the powers of the government. His mother, Anne of Austria, was made regent, and authorized to govern the country until the young king should arrive at a suitable age to exercise his hereditary powers in his own name. Anne of Austria had been always very kind to Henrietta, and had always rendered her assistance whenever she had been reduced to any special extremity of distress. It was she who had sent the supplies of money and clothing to Henrietta when she fled, sick and destitute, to Exeter, vainly hoping to find repose and the means of restoration there.

Besides King Louis XIII., who had died, Henrietta had another brother, whose name was Gaston, duke of Orleans. The Duke of Orleans had a daughter, who was styled the Duchess of Montpensier, deriving the title from her mother. She was, of course, also a cousin of Prince Charles. Her father, being brother of the late king, and uncle of the present one, was made lieutenant general of the kingdom, having thus the second place, that is, the place next to the queen, in the management of the affairs of the realm. Thus the little king commenced his reign by having in his court his mother as queen regent, his uncle lieutenant general, and his aunt, an exiled queen from a sister realm, his guest. He had also in his household his brother Philip, younger than himself, his cousin the young Duchess of Montpensier, and his cousin the Prince Charles. The family relationship of all these individuals will be made more clear by being presented in a tabular form, as follows:

Royal Family of France in the Time of Louis XIV.

	Louis XIII. Anne of Austria.	Louis XIV. Philip, 8 years old.
HENRY IV	Gaston, Duke of Orleans. Duchess of Montpensier.	Duchess of Montpensier
	Henrietta Maria. King Charles I.	Prince Charles, 16.

In the above table, the first column contains the name of Henry IV., the second those of three of his children, with the persons whom they respectively married, and the third the four grandchildren, who, as cousins, now found themselves domesticated together in the royal palaces of France.

The young king was, as has already been said, about eight years old at the time of Prince Charles's arrival. The palace in which he resided when in the city was the Palace Royal, which was then, and has been ever since, one of the most celebrated buildings in the world. It was built at an enormous expense, during a previous reign, by a powerful minister of state, who was, in ecclesiastical rank, a cardinal, and his mansion was named, accordingly, the Palace Cardinal. It had, however, been recently taken as a royal residence, and its name changed to Palace Royal. Here the queen regent had her grand apartments of state, every thing being as rich as the most lavish expenditure could make it. She had one apartment, called an oratory, a sort of closet for prayer, which was lighted by a large window, the sash of which was made of silver. The interior of the room was ornamented with the most costly paintings and furniture, and was enriched with a profusion of silver and gold. The little king had his range of apartments too, with a whole household of officers and attendants as little as himself. These children were occupied continually with ceremonies, and pageants, and mock military parades, in which they figured in miniature arms and badges of authority, and with dresses made to imitate those of real monarchs and ministers of state. Every thing was regulated with the utmost regard to etiquette and punctilio, and without any limits or bounds to the expense. Thus, though the youthful officers of the little monarch's household exercised no real power, they displayed all the forms and appearances of royalty with more than usual pomp and splendor. It was a species of child's play, it is true, but it was probably the most grand and magnificent child's play that the world has ever witnessed. It was into this extraordinary scene that Prince Charles found himself ushered on his arrival in France.

At the time of the prince's arrival the court happened to be residing, not at Paris, but at Fontainebleau. Fontainebleau, as has already been stated, is about forty miles from Paris, to the southward. There is a very splendid palace and castle there, built originally in very ancient times. There is a town near, both the castle and the town being in the midst of a vast park and forest, one of the most extended and magnificent royal domains in Europe. This forest has been reserved as a hunting ground for the French kings from a very early age. It covers an area of forty thousand acres, being thus many miles in extent. The royal family were at this palace at the time of Prince

49

Charles's arrival, celebrating the festivities of a marriage. The prince accordingly, as we shall presently see, went there to join them.

There were two persons who were anticipating the prince's arrival in France with special interest, his mother, and his young cousin, the Duchess of Montpensier. Her Christian name was Anne Marie Louisa.[2] She was a gay, frivolous, and coquettish girl, of about nineteen, immensely rich, being the heiress of the vast estates of her mother, who was not living. Her father, though he was the lieutenant general of the realm, and the former king's brother, was not rich. His wife, when she died, had bequeathed all her vast estates to her daughter Anne Maria was naturally haughty and vain, and; as her father was accustomed to come occasionally to her to get supplies of money, she was made vainer and more self-conceited still by his dependence upon her. Several matches had been proposed to her, and among them the Emperor of Germany had been named. He was a widower. His first wife, who had been Anne Maria's aunt, had just died. As the emperor was a potentate of great importance, the young belle thought she should prefer him to any of the others who had been proposed, and she made no secret of this her choice. It is true that he had made no proposal to her, but she presumed that he would do so after a suitable time had elapsed from the death of his first wife, and Anne Maria was contented to wait, considering the lofty elevation to which she would attain on becoming his bride.

But Queen Henrietta Maria had another plan. She was very desirous to obtain Anne Maria for the wife of her son Charles. There were many reasons for this. The young lady was a princess of the royal family of France; she possessed, too, an immense fortune, and was young and beautiful withal, though not quite so young as Charles himself. He was sixteen, and she was about nineteen. It is true that Charles was now, in some sense, a fugitive and an exile, destitute of property, and without a home. Still he was a prince. He was the heir apparent of the kingdoms of England and Scotland. He was young and accomplished. These high qualifications, somewhat exaggerated,

---

2   She is commonly called, in the annals of the day in which she lived, *Mademoiselle*, as she was, *par eminence*, the young lady of the court. In history she is commonly called Mademoiselle de Montpensier; we shall call her, in this narrative, simply Anne Maria, as that is, for our purpose, the most convenient designation.

perhaps, by maternal partiality, seemed quite sufficient to Henrietta to induce the proud duchess to become the prince's bride.

All this, it must be remembered, took place before the execution of King Charles the First, and when, of course, the fortunes of the family were not so desperate as they afterward became. Queen Henrietta had a great many conversations with Anne Maria before the prince arrived, in which she praised very highly his person and his accomplishments. She narrated to the duchess the various extraordinary adventures and the narrow escapes which the prince had met with in the course of his wanderings in England; she told her how dutiful and kind he had been to her as a son, and how efficient and courageous in his father's cause as a soldier. She described his appearance and his manners, and foretold how he would act, what tastes and preferences he would form, and how he would be regarded in the French court. The young duchess listened to all this with an appearance of indifference and unconcern, which was partly real and partly only assumed. She could not help feeling some curiosity to see her cousin, but her head was too full of the grander destination of being the wife of the emperor to think much of the pretensions of this wandering and homeless exile.

Prince Charles, on his arrival, went first to Paris, where he found his mother. There was an invitation for them here to proceed to Fontainebleau, where, as has already been stated, the young king and his court were now residing. They went there accordingly, and were received with every mark of attention and honor. The queen regent took the young king into the carriage of state, and rode some miles along the avenue, through the forest, to meet the prince and his mother when they were coming. They were attended with the usual cortege of carriages and horsemen, and they moved with all the etiquette and ceremony proper to be observed in the reception of royal visitors.

When the carriages met in the forest, they stopped, and the distinguished personages contained in them alighted. Queen Henrietta introduced her son to the queen regent and to Louis, the French king, and also to other personages of distinction who were in their train. Among them was Anne Maria. The queen regent took Henrietta and the prince into the carriage with her and the young king, and they proceeded thus together back to the palace. Prince Charles was somewhat embarrassed in making all these new acquaintances, in circumstances, too, of so much ceremony and parade, and the more so, as his knowledge of the French language was imperfect. He could understand it when spoken, but could not speak it well himself, and he appeared, accordingly, somewhat awkward and confused. He seemed particularly at a loss in his intercourse with Anne Maria. She was a little older than himself, and, being perfectly at home, both in the ceremonies of the occasion and in the language of the company, she felt entirely at her ease herself; and yet, from her natural temperament and character, she assumed such an air and bearing as would tend to prevent the prince from being so. In a word, it happened then as it has often happened since on similar occasions, that the beau was afraid of the belle.

The party returned to the palace. On alighting, the little king gave his hand to his aunt, the Queen of England, while Prince Charles gave his to the queen regent, and thus the two matrons were gallanted into the hall. The prince had a seat assigned him on the following day in the queen regent's drawing room, and was thus regularly instated as an inmate of the royal household. He remained here several days, and at length the whole party returned to Paris.

Anne Maria, in after years, wrote reminiscences of her early life, which were published after her death. In this journal she gives an account of her introduction to the young prince, and of her first acquaintance with him. It is expressed as follows:

"He was only sixteen or seventeen years of age, rather tall, with a fine head, black hair, a dark complexion, and a tolerably agreeable countenance. But he neither spoke nor understood French, which was very inconvenient. Nevertheless, every thing was done to amuse him, and, during the three days that he remained at Fontainebleau, there were hunts and every other sport which could be commanded in that season. He paid his respects to all the princesses, and I discovered immediately that the Queen of England wished to persuade me that he had fallen in love with me. She told me that he talked of me incessantly; that, were she not to prevent it, he would be in my apartment [3] at all hours; that he found me quite to his taste, and that he was in despair on account of the death of the empress, for he was afraid that they would seek to marry me to the emperor. I listened to all she said as became me, but it did not have as much effect upon me as probably she wished."

---

3   This means at her residence. The whole suite of rooms occupied by a family is called, in France, their *apartment*.

After spending a few days at Fontainebleau, the whole party returned to Paris, and Queen Henrietta and the prince took up their abode again in the Palace Royal, or, as it is now more commonly called, the Palais Royal. Charles was much impressed with the pomp and splendor of the French court, so different from the rough mode of life to which he had been accustomed in his campaigns and wanderings in England. The etiquette and formality, however, were extreme, every thing, even the minutest motions, being regulated by nice rules, which made social intercourse and enjoyment one perpetual ceremony. But, notwithstanding all this pomp and splendor, and the multitude of officers and attendants who were constantly on service, there seems to have been, in the results obtained, a strange mixture of grand parade with discomfort and disorder. At one time at Fontainebleau, at a great entertainment, where all the princes and potentates that had been drawn there by the wedding were assembled, the cooks quarreled in the kitchen, and one of the courses of the supper failed entirely in consequence of their dissensions; and at another time, as a large party of visitors were passing out through a suite of rooms in great state, to descend a grand staircase, where some illustrious foreigners, who were present, were to take their leave, they found the apartments through which they were to pass all dark. The servants had neglected or forgotten to light them.

These and similar incidents show that there may be regal luxury and state without order or comfort, as there may be regal wealth and power without any substantial happiness. Notwithstanding this, however, Prince Charles soon became strongly interested in the modes of life to which he was introduced at Paris and at Fontainebleau. There were balls, parties, festivities, and excursions of pleasure without number, his interest in these all being heightened by the presence of Anne Maria, whom he soon began to regard with a strong degree of that peculiar kind of interest which princesses and heiresses inspire. In Anne Maria's memoirs of her early life, we have a vivid description of many of the scenes in which both she herself and Charles were such prominent actors. She wrote always with great freedom, and in a very graphic manner, so that the tale which she tells of this period of her life forms a very entertaining narrative.

Anne Maria gives a very minute account of what took place between herself and Charles on several occasions in the course of their acquaintance, and describes particularly various balls, and parties, and excursions of pleasure on which she was attended by the young prince. Her vanity was obviously gratified by the interest which Charles seemed to take in her, but she was probably incapable of any feelings of deep and disinterested love, and Charles made no impression upon her heart. She reserved herself for the emperor.

For example, they were all one night invited to a grand ball by the Duchess de Choisy. This lady lived in a magnificent mansion, called the Hotel de Choisy. Just before the time came for the party of visitors to go, the Queen of England came over with Charles to the apartments of Anne Maria. The queen came ostensibly to give the last touches to the adjustment of the young lady's dress, and to the arrangement of her hair, but really, without doubt, in pursuance of her policy of taking every occasion to bring the young people together.

"She came," says Anne Maria, in her narrative, "to dress me and arrange my hair herself. She came for this purpose to my apartments, and took the utmost pains to set me off to the best advantage, and the Prince of Wales held the flambeau near me to light my toilet the whole time. I wore black, white, and carnation; and my jewelry was fastened by ribbons of the same colors. I wore a plume of the same kind; all these had been selected and ordered by my aunt Henrietta. The queen regent, who knew that I was in my aunt Henrietta's hands, sent for me to come and see her when I was all ready, before going to the ball. I accordingly went, and this gave the prince an opportunity to go at once to the Hotel de Choisy, and be ready there to receive me when I should arrive I found him there at the door, ready to hand me from my coach. I stopped in a chamber to readjust my hair, and the Prince of Wales again held a flambeau for me. This time, too, he brought his cousin, Prince Rupert, as an interpreter between us; for, believe it who will, though he could understand every word I said to him, he could not reply the least sentence to me in French. When the ball was finished and we retired, the prince followed me to the porter's lodge of my hotel,[4] and lingered till I entered, and then went his way.

---

4   In all the great houses in Paris, the principal buildings of the edifice stand back from the street, surrounding a court yard, which has sometimes shrubbery and flowers and a fountain in the center. The entrance to this court yard is by a great gate and archway on the street, with the apartments occupied by the *porter*, that is, the keeper of the gate, on one side. The entrance to the porter's lodge is from under the archway.

"There was another occasion on which his gallantry to me attracted a great deal of attention. It was at a great fete celebrated at the Palais Royal. There was a play acted, with scenery and music, and then a ball. It took three whole days to arrange my ornaments for this night. The Queen of England would dress me on this occasion, also, with her own hands. My robe was all figured with diamonds, with carnation trimmings. I wore the jewels of the crown of France, and, to add to them, the Queen of England lent me some fine ones of her own, which she had not then sold. The queen praised the fine turn of my shape, my air, the beauty of my complexion, and the brightness of my light hair. I had a conspicuous seat in the middle of the ballroom, with the young King of France and the Prince of Wales at my feet I did not feel the least embarrassed, for, as I had an idea of marrying the emperor, I regarded the Prince of Wales only as an object of pity."

Things went on in this way for a time, until at last some political difficulties occurred at Paris which broke in upon the ordinary routine of the royal family, and drove them, for a time, out of the city. Before these troubles were over, Henrietta and her son were struck down, as by a blow, by the tidings, which came upon them like a thunderbolt, that their husband and father had been beheaded. This dreadful event put a stop for a time to every thing like festive pleasures. The queen left her children, her palace, and all the gay circle of her friends, and retired to a convent, to mourn, in solitude and undisturbed, her irreparable loss.

VI

NEGOTIATIONS WITH ANNE MARIA

OUR Prince CHARLES now becomes, by the death of his father, King Charles the Second, both of England and of Scotland. That is, he becomes so in theory, according to the principles of the English Constitution, though, in fact, he is a fugitive and an exile still. Notwithstanding his exclusion, however, from the exercise of what he considered his right to reign, he was acknowledged as king by all true Royalists in England, and by all the continental powers. They would not aid him to recover his throne, but in the courts and royal palaces which he visited he was regarded as a king, and was treated, in form at least, with all the consideration and honor which belonged to royalty. Queen Henrietta was overwhelmed with grief and despair when she learned the dreadful tidings of the execution of her husband. At the time when these tidings came to her, she was involved, also, in many other sufferings and trials. As was intimated in the last chapter, serious difficulties had occurred between the royal family of France and the government and people of the city of Paris, from which a sort of insurrection had resulted, and the young king and his mother, together with all the principal personages of the court, had been compelled to fly from the city, in the night, to save their lives. They went in a train of twenty or thirty carriages, by torch light, having kept their plan a profound secret until the moment of their departure. The young king was asleep in his bed until the time arrived, when they took him up and put him into the carriage. Anne Maria, whose rank and wealth gave her a great deal of influence and power, took sides, in some degree, with the Parisians in this contest, so that her aunt, the queen regent, considered her as an enemy rather than a friend. She, however, took her with them in their flight; but Anne Maria, being very much out of humor, did all she could to tease and torment the party all the way. When they awoke her and informed her of their proposed escape from Paris, she was, as she says in her memoirs, very much delighted, for she knew that the movement was very unwise, and would get her aunt, the queen regent, and all their friends, into serious difficulties.

She dressed herself as quick as she could, came down stairs, and proceeded to enter the queen regent's coach, saying that she wanted to have one or the other of certain seats—naming the best places—as she had no idea, she said, of being exposed to cold, or riding uncomfortably on such a night. The queen told her that those seats were for herself and another lady of high rank who was with her, to which Anne Maria replied, "Oh, very well; I suppose young ladies ought to give up to *old* people."

In the course of conversation, as they were preparing to ride away, the queen asked Anne Maria if she was not surprised at being called up to go on such an expedition. "Oh no," said she; "my father" (that is, Gaston, the duke of Orleans) "told me all about it beforehand." This was not true, as she says herself in her own account of these transactions. She knew nothing about the plan until she was called from her bed. She said this, therefore, only to tease her aunt by the false pretension that the secret had been confided to her. Her aunt, however, did not believe her, and said, "Then why did you go to bed, if you knew what was going on?" "Oh," replied Anne Maria, "I thought it would be a good plan to get some sleep, as I did not know whether I should even have a bed to lie upon to-morrow night."

The party of fugitives exhibited a scene of great terror and confusion, as they were assembling and crowding into their carriages, before they left the court of the Palais Royal. It was past midnight, in the month of January, and there was no moon. Called up suddenly as they were from their beds, and frightened with imaginary dangers, they all pressed forward, eager to go; and so hurried was their departure, that they took with them very scanty supplies, even for their most ordinary wants. At length they drove away. They passed rapidly out of the city. They proceeded to an ancient palace and castle called St. Germain's, about ten miles northeast of Paris. Anne

Maria amused herself with the fears, and difficulties, and privations which the others suffered, and she gives an account of the first night they spent in the place of their retreat, which, as it illustrates her temperament and character, the reader will like perhaps, to see.

"I slept in a very handsome room, well painted, well gilded, and large, with very little fire, and no windows,[5] which is not very agreeable in the month of January. I slept on mattresses, which were laid upon the floor, and my sister, who had no bed, slept with me. I was obliged to sing to get her to sleep, and then her slumber did not last long, so that she disturbed mine. She tossed about, felt me near her, woke up, and exclaimed that she saw the beast, so I was obliged to sing again to put her to sleep, and in that way I passed the night. Judge whether this was an agreeable situation for one who had had little or no sleep the night before, and who had been ill all winter with colds. However, the fatigue and exposure of this expedition cured me.

"In a short time my father gave me his room, but as nobody knew I was there, I was awoke in the night by a noise. I drew back my curtain, and was astonished to find my chamber filled with men in large buff skin collars, and who appeared surprised to see me, and knew me as little as I did them. I had no change of linen, and when I wanted any thing washed, it was done in the night, while I was in bed. I had no women to arrange my hair and dress me, which is very inconvenient. Still I did not lose my gayety, and they were in admiration at my making no complaint; and it is true that I am a creature that can make the most of every thing, and am greatly above trifles."

To feel any commiseration for this young lady, on account of the alarm which she may be supposed to have experienced at seeing all those strange men in her chamber, would be sympathy thrown away, for her nerves were not of a sensibility to be affected much by such a circumstance as that. In fact, as the difficulties between the young king's government and the Parisians increased, Anne Maria played quite the part of a heroine. She went back and forth to Paris in her carriage, through the mob, when nobody else dared to go. She sometimes headed troops, and escorted ladies and gentlemen when they were afraid to go alone. Once she relieved a town, and once she took the command of the cannon of the Bastille, and issued her or-

---

5   That is, with no glass to the windows.

ders to fire with it upon the troops, with a composure which would have done honor to any veteran officer of artillery. We can not go into all these things here in detail, as they would lead us too far away from the subject of this narrative. We only allude to them, to give our readers some distinct idea of the temperament and character of the rich and blooming beauty whom young King Charles was wishing so ardently to make his bride.

During the time that these difficulties continued in Paris, Queen Henrietta's situation was extremely unhappy. She was shut up in the palace of the Louvre, which became now her prison rather than her home. She was separated from the royal family; her son, the king, was generally absent in Holland or in Jersey, and her palace was often surrounded by mobs; whenever she ventured out in her carriage, she was threatened with violence and outrage by the populace in such a manner as to make her retreat as soon as possible to the protection of the palace walls. Her pecuniary means, too, were exhausted. She sold her jewels, from time to time, as long as they lasted, and then contracted debts which her creditors were continually pressing her to pay. Her friends at St. Germain's could not help her otherwise than by asking her to come to them. This she at last concluded to do, and she made her escape from Paris, under the escort of Anne Maria, who came to the city for the purpose of conducting her, and who succeeded, though with infinite difficulty, in securing a safe passage for Henrietta through the crowds of creditors and political foes who threatened to prevent her journey. These troubles were all, however, at last settled, and in the autumn (1649) the whole party returned again to Paris.

In the mean time the young King Charles was contriving schemes for getting possession of his realm. It will be recollected that his sister Mary, who married the Prince of Orange, was at this time residing at the Hague, a city in Holland, near the sea. Charles went often there. It was a sort of rendezvous for those who had been obliged to leave England on account of their attachment to his father's fortunes, and who, now that the father was dead, transferred their loyalty to the son. They felt a very strong desire that Charles's plans for getting possession of his kingdom should succeed, and they were willing to do every thing in their power to promote his success. It must not be supposed, however, that they were governed in this by a disinterested principle of fidelity to Charles himself personally, or to the justice of his cause. Their own re-establishment in wealth and power was at stake as well as his, and they were ready to make common cause with him, knowing that they could save themselves from ruin only by reinstating him.

Charles had his privy council and a sort of court at the Hague, and he arranged channels of communication, centering there, for collecting intelligence from England and Scotland, and through these he watched in every way for the opening of an opportunity to assert his rights to the British crown. He went, too, to Jersey, where the authorities and the inhabitants were on his side, and both there and at the Hague he busied himself with plans for raising funds and levying troops, and securing co-operation from those of the people of England who still remained loyal. Ireland was generally in his favor too, and he seriously meditated an expedition there. His mother was unwilling to have him engage in these schemes. She was afraid he would, sooner or later, involve himself in dangers from which he could not extricate himself, and that he would end by being plunged into the same pit of destruction that had engulfed his father.

Amid all these political schemes, however, Charles did not forget Anne Maria. He was sager to secure her for his bride; for her fortune, and the power and influence of her connections, would aid him very much in recovering his throne. Her hope of marrying the Emperor of Germany, too, was gone, for that potentate had chosen another wife. Charles therefore continued his attentions to the young lady. She would not give him any distinct and decisive answer, but kept the subject in a state of perpetual negotiation. She was, in fact, growing more and more discontented and unhappy in disposition all the time. Her favorite plan of marrying the emperor had been thwarted, in part, by the difficulties which her friends—her father and her aunt especially—had contrived secretly to throw in the way, while outwardly and ostensibly they appeared to be doing all in their power to promote her wishes. They did not wish to have her married at all, as by this event the management of her vast fortune would pass out of their hands. She discovered this, their double dealing, when it was too late, and she was overwhelmed with vexation and chagrin.

Things being in this state, Charles sent a special messenger, at one time, from the Hague, with instructions to make a formal proposal to Anne Maria, and to see if he could not bring the affair to a close. The name of this messenger was Lord Germain. The queen regent and her father urged Anne Maria now to consent to the proposal. They told her that Charles's prospects were brightening—that they themselves were going to render him powerful protection—that he had already acquired several allies—that there were whole provinces in England that were in his favor; and that all Ireland, which was, as it were, a kingdom in itself, was on his side. Whether they seriously desired that Anne Maria would consent to Charles's proposals, or only urged, for effect, what they knew very well she would persist in refusing, it is impossible to ascertain. If this latter were their design, it seemed likely to fail, for Anne Maria appeared to yield. She was sorry, she said, that the situation of affairs in Paris was not such as to allow of the French government giving Charles effectual help in gaining possession of the throne; but still, not withstanding that, she was ready to do what ever they might think best to command.

Lord Germain then said that he should proceed directly to Holland and escort Charles to France, and he wanted Anne Maria to give him a direct and positive reply; for if she would really accept his proposal, he would come at once to court and claim her as his bride; otherwise he must proceed to Ireland, for the state of his affairs demanded his presence there. But if she would accept his proposal, he would immediately come to Paris, and have the marriage ceremony performed, and then he would remain afterward some days with her, that she might enjoy the honors and distinctions to which she would become entitled as the queen consort of a mighty realm. He would then, if she liked the plan, take her to Saint Germain's, where his mother, her aunt, was then residing, and establish her there while he was recovering his kingdom; or, if she preferred it, she might take up her residence in Paris, where she had been accustomed to live.

To this the young lady replied that the last mentioned plan, that is, that she should continue to live at Paris after being married to Charles, was one that she could not think of. She should feel altogether unwilling to remain and enjoy the gayeties and festivities of Paris while her husband was at the head of his armies, exposed to all the dangers and privations of a camp; nor should she consider it right to go on incurring the expenses which a lady of her rank and position must necessarily bear in such a city, while he was perhaps embarrassed and distressed with the difficulties of providing funds for his own and his followers' necessities. She should feel, in fact, bound, if she were to become his wife, to do all in her power to assist him; and it would end, she foresaw, in her having to dispose of all her property, and expend the avails in aiding him to recover his kingdom. This, she said, she confessed alarmed her. It was a great sacrifice for her to make, reared as she had been in opulence and luxury. Lord Germain replied that all this was doubtless true, but then, on the other hand, he would venture to remind her that there was no other suitable match for her in Europe. He then went on to name the principal personages. The Emperor of Germany and the King of Spain were both married. Some other monarch was just about to espouse a Spanish princess. Others whom he named were too young; others, again, too old; and a certain prince whom he mentioned had been married, he said, these ten years, and his wife was in excellent health, so that every species of hope seemed to be cut off in that quarter.

This conversation leading to no decisive result, Lord Germain renewed the subject after a few days, and pressed Anne Maria for a final answer. She said, now, that she had a very high regard for Queen Henrietta, and, indeed, a very strong affection for her; so strong that she should be willing to waive, for Henrietta's sake, all her objections to the disadvantages of Charles's position; but there was one objection which she felt that she could not surmount, and that was his religion. He was a Protestant, while she was a Catholic. Charles must remove this difficulty himself, which, if he had any regard for her, he certainly would be willing to do, since she would have to make so many sacrifices for him. Lord Germain, however, immediately discouraged this idea. He said that the position of Charles in respect to his kingdom was such as to render it impossible for him to change his religious faith. In fact, if he were to do so, he would be compelled to give up, at once, all hope of ever getting possession of his throne. Anne Maria knew this very well. The plea, however, made an excellent excuse to defend herself with from Lord Germain's importunities. She adhered to it, therefore, pertinaciously; the negotiation was broken off, and Lord Germain went away.

Young adventurers like Charles, who wish to marry great heiresses, have always to exercise a great deal of patience, and to submit to a great many postponements and delays, even though they are successful in the end; and sovereign princes are not excepted, any more than other men, from this necessity. Dependent as woman is during all the earlier and all the later years of her life, and subjected as she is to the control, and too often, alas! to the caprice and injustice of man, there is a period—brief, it is true—when she is herself in power; and such characters as Anne Maria like to exercise their authority, while they feel that they possess it, with a pretty high hand. Charles seems to have felt the necessity of submitting to the inconvenience of Anne Maria's capricious delays, and, as long as she only continued to make excuses and objections instead of giving him a direct and positive refusal, he was led to persevere. Accordingly, not long after the conversations which his messenger had held with the lady as already described, he determined to come himself to France, and see if he could not accomplish something by his own personal exertions. He accordingly advanced to Peronne, which was not far from the frontier, and sent forward a courier to announce his approach. The royal family concluded to go out in their carriages to meet him. They were at this time at a famous royal resort a few leagues from Paris, called Compiegne. Charles was to dine at Compiegne, and then to proceed on toward Paris, where he had business to transact connected with his political plans.

Anne Maria gives a minute account of the ride of the royal family to meet Charles on his approach to Compiegne, and of the interview with him, on her part, which attended it. She dressed herself in the morning, she says, with great care, and had her hair curled, which she seldom did except on very special occasions. When she entered the carriage to go out to meet the king, the queen regent, observing her appearance, said archly, "How easy it is to tell when young ladies expect to meet their lovers." Anne Maria says that she had a great mind to tell her, in reply, that it *was* easy, for those who had had a great deal of experience in preparing to meet lovers themselves. She did not, however, say this, and the forbearance seems to show that there was, after all, the latent element of discretion and respect for superiors in her character, though it showed itself so seldom in action.

They rode out several miles to meet the coming king; and when the two parties met, they all alighted, and saluted each other by the road side, the ladies and gentlemen that accompanied them standing around. Anne Maria noticed that Charles addressed the king and queen regent first, and then her. After a short delay they got into their carriages again—King Charles entering the carriage with their majesties and Anne Maria—and they rode together thus back to Compiegne.

Anne Maria, however, does not seem to have been in a mood to be pleased. She says that Charles began to talk with the king—Louis XIV.—who was now twelve years old, about the dogs and horses, and the hunting customs in the country of the Prince of Orange. He talked on these subjects fluently enough in the French language, but when afterward the queen regent, who would naturally be interested in a different class of topics, asked him about the affairs of his own kingdom and his plans for recovering it, he excused himself by saying that he did not speak French well enough to give her the information. Anne Maria says she determined from that moment not to conclude the marriage, "for I conceived a very poor opinion of him, being a king, and at his age, to have no knowledge of his affairs." Such minds as Anne Maria's are seldom very logical; but such an inference as this, that he was ignorant of his own affairs because he declined explaining plans whose success depended on secrecy in such a company as that, and in a language with which, though he could talk about dogs and horses in it, he was still very imperfectly acquainted, is far too great a jump from premises to conclusion to be honestly made. It is very evident that Anne Maria was not disposed to be pleased.

They arrived at Compiegne. As the king was going on that evening, dinner was served soon after they arrived. Anne Maria says he ate no ortolans, a very expensive and rare dish of little birds, which had been prepared expressly for this dinner in honor of the royal guest,[6] "but flung himself upon a piece of beef and a shoulder of mutton, as if there had been nothing else at table. After dinner, when we were in the drawing room, the queen amused herself with the other ladies and gentlemen, and left him with me. He was a quarter of an hour without speaking a word; but I am willing to believe that his silence was the result of respect rather than any want of passion, though on this occasion, I frankly confess, I could have

---

6   The ortolan is a very small bird, which is fattened in lamp lighted rooms
     at great expense, because it is found to be of a more delicate flavor when
     excluded from the daylight. They come from the island of Cyprus, and have
     been famous in every age of the world as an article of royal luxury.

wished it less plainly exhibited. After a while, getting tired of his tediousness, I called another lady to my side, to see if she could not make him talk. She succeeded. Presently one of the gentlemen of the party came to me and said, 'He kept looking at you all dinner time, and is looking at you still.' To which I replied, 'He has plenty of time to look at me before he will please me, if he does not speak.' The gentleman rejoined, 'Oh, he has said tender things enough to you, no doubt, only you don't like to admit it.' To which I answered, 'Come and seat yourself by me the next time he is at my side, and hear for yourself how he talks about it." She says she then went and addressed the king herself, asking him various questions about persons who were in his suite, and that he answered them all with an air of mere common politeness, without any gallantry at all.

Finally, the hour for the departure of Charles and his party arrived, and the carriages came to the door. The French king, together with his mother and Anne Maria, and the usual attendants, accompanied them some miles into the forest on their way, and then, all alighting, as they had done when they met in the morning, they took leave of each other with the usual ceremonies of such occasions. Charles, after bidding King Louis farewell, advanced with Lord Germain, who was present in his suite at that time, to Anne Maria, and she gives the following rather petulant account of what passed: "'I believe,' said Charles, 'that my Lord Germain, who speaks French better than I do, has explained to you my sentiments and my intention. I am your very obedient servant.' I answered that I was equally his obedient servant. Germain paid me a great number of compliments, the king standing by. After they were over, the king bowed and departed."

Charles, who had been all his life living roughly in camps, felt naturally ill at ease in the brilliant scenes of ceremony and splendor which the French court presented; and this embarrassment was greatly increased by the haughty air and manner, and the ill concealed raillery of the lady whose favorable regard he was so anxious to secure. His imperfect knowledge of the language, and his sense of the gloomy uncertainty of his own prospects in life, tended strongly to increase his distrust of himself and his timidity. We should have wished that he could have experienced somewhat kinder treatment from the object of his regard, were it not that his character, and especially his subsequent history, show that he was entirely mercenary and selfish himself in seeking her hand. If we can ever, in any instance, pardon the caprice and wanton cruelty of a coquette, it is when these qualities are exercised in thwarting the designs of a heartless speculator, who is endeavoring to fill his coffers with money by offering in exchange for it a mere worthless counterfeit of love.

Charles seems to have been totally discouraged by the result of this unfortunate dinner party at Compiegne. He went to Paris, and from Paris he went to St. Germain's, where he remained for several months with his mother, revolving in his mind his fallen fortunes, and forming almost hopeless schemes for seeking to restore them. In the mean time, the wife whom the Emperor of Germany had married instead of Anne Maria, died, and the young belle sprang immediately into the excitement of a new hope of attaining the great object of her ambition after all. The emperor was fifty years of age, and had four children, but he was the Emperor of Germany, and that made amends for all. Anne Maria immediately began to lay her trains again for becoming his bride. What her plans were, and how they succeeded, we shall, perhaps, have occasion hereafter to describe.

Though her heart was thus set upon having the emperor for her husband, she did not like, in the mean time, quite to give up her younger and more agreeable beau. Besides, her plans of marrying the emperor might fail, and Charles might succeed in recovering his kingdom. It was best, therefore, not to bring the negotiation with him to too absolute a close. When the time arrived, therefore, for Charles to take his departure, she thought she would just ride out to St. Germain's and pay her respects to Queen Henrietta, and bid the young king good-by.

Neither Queen Henrietta nor her son attempted to renew the negotiation of his suite on the occasion of this visit. The queen told Anne Maria, on the other hand, that she supposed she ought to congratulate her on the death of the Empress of Germany, for, though the negotiation for her marriage with him had failed on a former occasion, she had no doubt it would be resumed now, and would be successful. Anne Maria replied, with an air of indifference, that she did not know or think any thing about it. The queen then said that she knew of a young man, not very far from them, who thought that a king of nineteen years of age was better for a husband than a man of fifty, a widower with four children, even if he was an emperor.

"However," said she, "we do not know what turn things may take. My son may succeed in recovering his kingdom, and then, perhaps, if you should be in a situation to do so, you may listen more favorably to his addresses."

Anne Maria was not to return directly back to Paris. She was going to visit her sisters, who lived at a little distance beyond. The Duke of York, that is, Henrietta's son James, then fourteen or fifteen years old, proposed to accompany her. She consented. Charles then proposed to go too. Anne Maria objected to this, saying that it was not quite proper. She had no objection to James's going, as he was a mere youth. Queen Henrietta removed her objection by offering to join the party herself; so they all went together. Anne Maria says that Charles treated her with great politeness and attention all the way, and paid her many compliments, but made no attempt to bring up again, in any way, the question of his suit. She was very glad he did not, she says, for her mind being now occupied with the plan of marrying the emperor, nothing that he could have said would have done any good.

Thus the question was considered as virtually settled, and King Charles, soon after, turned his thoughts toward executing the plans which he had been long revolving for the recovery of his kingdom.

VII

THE ROYAL OAK OF BOSCOBEL

I T was in June, 1650, about eighteen months after the decapitation of his father, that Charles was ready to set out on his expedition to attempt the recovery of his rights to the English throne. He was but twenty years of age. He took with him no army, no supplies, no resources. He had a small number of attendants and followers, personally interested themselves in his success, and animated also, probably, by some degree of disinterested attachment to him. It was, however, on the whole, a desperate enterprise. Queen Henrietta, in her retirement at the Louvre, felt very anxious about the result of it. Charles himself, too, notwithstanding his own buoyant and sanguine temperament, and the natural confidence and hope pertaining to his years, must have felt many forebodings. But his condition on the Continent was getting every month more and more destitute and forlorn. He was a mere guest wherever he went, and destitute of means as he was, he found himself continually sinking in public consideration. Money as well as rank is very essentially necessary to make a relative a welcome guest, for any long time, in aristocratic circles. Charles concluded, therefore, that, all things considered, it was best for him to make a desperate effort to recover his kingdoms.

His kingdoms were three, England, Scotland, and Ireland. Ireland was a conquered kingdom, Scotland, like England, had descended to him from his ancestors; for his grandfather, James VI., was king of Scotland, and being on his mothers side a descendant of an English king, he was, of course, one of the heirs of the English crown; and on the failure of the other heirs, he succeeded to that crown, retaining still his own. Thus both kingdoms descended to Charles.

It was only the English kingdom that had really rebelled against, and put to death King Charles's father. There had been a great deal of difficulty in Scotland, it is true, and the republican spirit had spread quite extensively in that country. Still, affairs had not proceeded to such extremities there. The Scotch had, in some degree, joined with the English in resisting Charles the First, but it was not their wish to throw off the royal authority altogether. They abhorred episcopacy in the Church, but were well enough contented with monarchy in the state. Accordingly, soon after the death of the father, they had opened negotiations with the son, and had manifested their willingness to acknowledge him as their king, on certain conditions which they undertook to prescribe to him. It is very hard for a king to hold his scepter on conditions prescribed by his people. Charles tried every possible means to avoid submitting to this necessity. He found, however, that the only possible avenue of access to England was by first getting some sort of possession of Scotland; and so, signifying his willingness to comply with the Scotch demands, he set sail from Holland with his court, moved north ward with his little squadron over the waters of the German Ocean, and at length made port In the Frith of Cromarty, in the north of Scotland.

The Scotch government, having but little faith in the royal word of such a youth as Charles would not allow him to land until he had formally signed their covenant, by which he bound himself to the conditions which they had thought it necessary to impose. He then landed. But he found his situation very far from such as comported with his ideas of royal authority and state. Charles was a gay, dissipated, reckless young man. The men whom he had to deal with were stern, sedate, and rigid religionists. They were scandalized at the looseness and irregularity of his character and manners. He was vexed and tormented by what he considered their ascetic bigotry, by the restraints which they were disposed to put upon his conduct, and the limits with which they insisted on bounding his authority. Long negotiations and debates ensued, each party becoming more and more irritated against the other. At last, on one occasion, Charles lost his patience entirely, and made his escape into the mountains, in hopes to raise an army there among the clans of wild Highlanders, who, accustomed from infancy to the most implicit obedience to their chieftains, are always very loyal to their king. The Scotch nobles, however, not wishing to drive him to extremities, sent for him to come back, and both parties becoming after this somewhat more considerate and accommodating, they at length came to an agreement, and proceeding together to Scone, a village some miles north of Edinburgh, they crowned Charles King of Scotland in a venerable abbey there, the ancient place of coronation for all the monarchs of the Scottish line.

In the mean time, Cromwell, who was at the head of the republican government of England, knowing very well that Charles's plan would be to march into England as soon as he could mature his arrangements for such an enterprise, determined to anticipate this design by declaring war himself against Scotland, and marching an army there.

Charles felt comparatively little interest in what became of Scotland. His aim was England. He knew, or supposed that there was a very large portion of the English people who secretly favored his cause, and he believed that if he could once cross the frontier, even with a small army, these his secret friends would all rise at once and flock to his standard. Still he attempted for a time to resist Cromwell in Scotland, but without success. Cromwell penetrated to the heart of the country, and actually passed the army of Charles. In these circumstances, Charles resolved to leave Scotland to its fate, and boldly to cross the English frontier, to see what he could do by raising his standard in his southern kingdom. The army acceded to this plan with acclamations. The king accordingly put his forces in motion, crossed the frontier, issued his manifestoes, and sent around couriers and heralds, announcing to the whole population that their king had come, and summoning all his subjects to arm themselves and hasten to his aid. This was in the summer of 1651, the year after his landing in Scotland.

It certainly was a very bold and almost desperate measure, and the reader, whether Monarchist or Republican, can hardly help wishing the young adventurer success. The romantic enterprise was, however, destined to fail. The people of England were not yet prepared to return to royalty. Some few of the ancient noble families and country gentlemen adhered to the king's cause, but they came in to join his ranks very slowly. Those who were in favor of the king were called *Cavaliers*. The other party were called *Roundheads*. Queen Henrietta Maria had given them the name, on account of their manner of wearing their hair, cut short and close to their heads all around, while the gay Cavaliers cultivated their locks, which hung in long curls down upon their shoulders. The Cavaliers, it turned out, were few, while the Roundheads filled the land.

It was, however, impossible for Charles to retreat, since Cromwell was behind him; for Cromwell, as soon as he found that his enemy had actually gone into England, paused only long enough to recover from his surprise, and then made all haste to follow him. The two armies thus moved down through the very heart of England, carrying every where, as they went, universal terror, confusion, and dismay. The whole country was thrown into extreme excitement. Every body was called upon to take sides, and thousands were perplexed and undecided which side to take. Families were divided, brothers separated, fathers and sons were ready to fight each other in their insane zeal, the latter for the Parliament, the former for the king. The whole country was filled with rumors, messengers, parties of soldiers going to and fro, and troops of horsemen, with robberies, plunderings, murders, and other deeds of violence without number, and all the other elements of confusion and misery which arouse the whole population of a country to terror and distress, and mar the very face of nature in time of civil war. What dreadful struggles man will make to gain the pleasure of ruling his fellow man! Along the frontiers of England and Wales there flows the beautiful River Severn, which widens majestically at its mouth, and passes by the Bristol Channel to the sea. One of the largest towns upon this river is Worcester. It was in those days strongly fortified. It stands on the eastern side of the river, with a great bridge opposite one of the gates leading across the Severn in the direction toward Wales. There are other bridges on the stream, both above and below, and many towns and villages in the vicinity, the whole presenting, at ordinary times, a delightful scene of industry and peace.

Worcester is, perhaps, three hundred miles from the frontiers of Scotland, on the way to London, though somewhat to the westward of the direct route. Charles's destination was the capital. He pushed on, notwithstanding the difficulties and disappointments which embarrassed his march, until at last, when he reached the banks of the Severn, he found he could go no further. His troops and his officers were wearied, faint, and discouraged. His hopes had not been realized, and while it was obviously dangerous to stop, it seemed still more dangerous to go on. However, as the authorities of Worcester were disposed to take sides with the king, Charles determined to stop there for a little time, at all events, to refresh his army, and consider what to do.

He was received in the city with all due honors. He was proclaimed king on the following day, with great parade and loud acclamations. He established a camp in the neighborhood of the city. He issued great proclamations, calling upon all the people of the surrounding country to come and espouse his cause. He established his court, organized his privy council, and, in a word, perfected, on a somewhat humble scale it is true, all the arrangements proper to the condition of a monarch in his capital. He began, perhaps, in fact, to imagine himself really a king. If he did so, however, the illusion was soon dispelled. In one short week Cromwell's army came on, filling all the avenues of approach to the city, and exhibiting a force far too great, apparently, either for Charles to meet in battle, or to defend himself from in a siege.

Charles's forces fought several preliminary battles and skirmishes in resisting the attempts of Cromwell's columns to get possession of the bridges and fords by which they were to cross the river. These contests resulted always in the same way. The detachments which Charles had sent forward to defend these points were one after another driven in, while Charles, with his council of war around him, watched from the top of the tower of a church within the city this gradual and irresistible advance of his determined enemy, with an anxiety which gradually deepened into dismay.

The king, finding his situation now desperate, determined to make one final attempt to retrieve his fallen fortunes. He formed his troops in array, and marched out to give the advancing army battle. He put himself at the head of a troop of Highlanders, and fought in person with the courage and recklessness of despair. The officers knew full well that it was a question of victory or death; for if they did not conquer, they must die, either by wounds on the field of battle, or else, if taken prisoners, by being hung as traitors, or beheaded in the Tower. All possibility of escape, entrapped and surrounded as they were in the very heart of the country, hundreds of miles from the frontiers, seemed utterly hopeless. They fought, therefore, with reckless and desperate fury, but all was in vain. They were repulsed and driven in on all sides, and the soldiers fled at length, carrying the officers with them, in tumult and disorder, back through the gates into the city. An army flying in confusion to seek refuge in a city can not shut the gates behind them against their pursuers. In fact, in such a scene of terror and dismay, there is no order, no obedience, no composure. At the gate where Charles endeavored to get back into the city, he found the way choked up by a heavy ammunition cart which had been entangled there, one of the oxen that had been drawing it being killed. The throngs of men &and horsemen were stopped by this disaster. The king dismounted, abandoned his horse, and made his way through and over the obstruction as he could. When he got into the city, he found all in confusion there. His men were throwing away their arms, and pressing onward in their flight. He lightened his own burdens by laying aside the heaviest of his armor, procured another horse, and rode up and down among his men, urging and entreating them to form again and face the enemy. He plead the justice of his cause, their duty to be faithful to their rightful sovereign, and every other argument which was capable of being expressed in the shouts and vociferations which, in such a scene, constitute the only kind of communication possible with panic stricken men; and when he found that all was in vain he said, in despair, that he would rather they would shoot him on the spot than let him live to witness such an abandonment of his cause by the only friends and followers that had been left to him.

The powerful influence which these expostulations would otherwise have had, was lost and overborne in the torrent of confusion and terror which was spreading through all the streets of the city. The army of Cromwell forced their passage in, and fought their way from street to street, wherever they found any remaining resistance. Some of the king's troops were hemmed up in corners, and cut to pieces. Others, somewhat more fortunate, sought protection in towers and bastions, where they could make some sort of conditions with their victorious enemy before surrendering. Charles himself, finding that all was lost, made his escape at last from the city, at six o'clock in the evening, at the head of a troop of horse. He could not, however, endure the thought of giving up the contest, after all. Again and again, as he slowly retreated, he stopped to face about, and to urge his men to consent to turn back again and encounter the enemy. Their last halt was upon a bridge half a mile from the city. Here the king held a consultation with the few remaining counselors and officers that were with him, surveying, with them, the routed and flying bodies of men, who were now throwing away their arms and dispersing in all directions, in a state of hopeless disorganization and despair. The king saw plainly that his cause was irretrievably ruined, and they all agreed that nothing now remained for them but to make their escape back to Scotland, if by any possibility that could now be done.

But how should they accomplish this end? To follow the multitude of defeated soldiers would be to share the certain capture and death which awaited them, and they were themselves all strangers to the country. To go on inquiring all the way would only expose them to equally certain discovery and capture. The first thing, however, obviously was to get away from the crowd. Charles and his attendants, therefore, turned aside from the high road—there were with the king fifty or sixty officers and noblemen, all mounted men—and moved along in such secluded by-paths as they could find. The king wished to diminish even this number of followers, but he could not get any of them to leave him. He complained afterward, in the account which he gave of these adventures, that, though they would not fight for him when battle was to be given, he could not get rid of them when the time came for flight.

There was a servant of one of the gentlemen in the company who pretended to know the way, and he accordingly undertook to guide the party; but as soon as it became dark he got confused and lost, and did not know what to do. They contrived, however, to get another guide They went ten miles, attracting no particular attention, for at such a time of civil war a country is full of parties of men, armed and unarmed, going to and fro, who are allowed generally to move without molestation, as the inhabitants are only anxious to have as little as possible to say to them, that they may the sooner be gone. The royal party assumed the air and manner of one of these bands as long as daylight lasted, and when that was gone they went more securely and at their ease. After proceeding ten miles, they stopped at an obscure inn, where they took some drink and a little bread, and then resumed their journey, consulting with one another as they went as to what it was best to do.

About ten or twelve miles further on there was a somewhat wild and sequestered region, in which there were two very secluded dwellings, about half a mile from each other. One of these residences was named Boscobel. The name had been given to it by a guest of the proprietor, at an entertainment which the latter had given, from the Italian words *bosco bello*, which mean beautiful grove. It was in or near a wood, and away from all high roads, having been built, probably, like many other of the dwellings reared in those days, as a place of retreat. In the preceding reigns of Charles and Elizabeth, the Catholics, who were called *popish recusants*, on account of their *refusing* to take an oath acknowledging the supremacy of the British sovereign over the English Church, had to resort to all possible modes of escape from Protestant persecution. They built these retreats in retired and secluded places, and constructed all sorts of concealed and secure hiding places within them, in the partitions and walls, where men whose lives were in danger might be concealed for many days. Boscobel was such a mansion. In fact, one of the king's generals, the Earl of Derby, had been concealed in it but a short time before. The king inquired particularly about it, and was induced himself to seek refuge there.

This house belonged to a family of Giffards, one of whom was in the suite of King Charles at this time. There was another mansion about half a mile distant. This other place had been originally, in the Catholic days, a convent, and the nuns who inhabited it dressed in white. They were called, accordingly, the *white ladies*, and the place itself received the same name, which it retained after the sisters were gone. Mr. Giffard recommended going to the White Ladies' first. He wanted, in fact, to contrive some way to relieve the king of the encumbrance of so large a troop before going to Boscobel.

They went, accordingly, to the White Ladies'. Neither of the houses was occupied at this time by the proprietors, but were in charge of housekeepers and servants. Among the tenants upon the estate there were several brothers of the name of Penderel. They were woodmen and farm servants, living at different places in the neighborhood, and having charge, some of them, of the houses above described. One of the Penderels was at the White Ladies'. He let the fugitives in, tired, exhausted, and hungry as they were, with the fatigue of marching nearly all the night. They sent immediately for Richard Penderel, who lived in a farm house nearby, and for another brother, who was at Boscobel. They took the king into an inner room, and immediately commenced the work of effectually disguising him.

They gave him clothes belonging to some of the servants of the family, and destroyed his own. The king had about his person a watch and some costly decorations, such as orders of knighthood set in jewels, which would betray his rank if found in his possession. These the king distributed among his friends, intrusting them to the charge of such as he judged most likely to effect their escape. They then cut off his hair short all over, thus making him a Roundhead instead of a Cavalier. They rubbed soot from the fire place over his face, to change the expression of his features and complexion. They gave him thus, in all respects, as nearly as possible, the guise of a squalid peasant and laborer of the humblest class, accustomed to the privations and to the habits of poverty.

In the mean time Richard Penderel arrived. Perhaps an intimation had been given him of the wishes of the king to be relieved of his company of followers; at any rate, he urged the whole retinue, as soon as he came to the house to press forward without any delay, as there was a detachment of Cromwell's forces, he said, at three miles' distance, who might be expected at any moment to come in pursuit of them Giffard brought Penderel then into the inner room to which the king had retired. "This is the king," said he. "I commit him to your charge. Take care of him."

Richard undertook the trust. He told the king that he must immediately leave that place, and he conducted him secretly, all disguised as he was, out of a postern door, without making known his design to any of his followers, except the two or three who were in immediate attendance upon him. He led him away about half a mile into a wood, and, concealing him there, left him alone, saying he would go and see what intelligence he could obtain, and presently return again. The troop of followers, in the mean time, from whom the king had been so desirous to get free, when they found that he was gone, mounted their horses and rode away, to escape the danger with which Richard had threatened them. But, alas for the unhappy fugitives, they did not get far in their flight; they were overtaken, attacked, conquered, captured, and treated as traitors. Some were shot, one was beheaded, and others were shut up in prisons, where they pined in hopeless privation and suffering for many years. There was, however, one of the king's followers who did not go away with the rest. It was Lord Wilmot, an influential nobleman, who concealed himself in the vicinity, and kept near the king in all his subsequent wanderings.

But we must return to the king in the wood. It was about sunrise when he was left there, the morning after the battle. It rained. The king tried in vain to find a shelter under the trees of the forest. The trees themselves were soon thoroughly saturated, and they received the driving rain from the skies only to let the water fall in heavier drops upon the poor fugitive's defenseless head. Richard borrowed a blanket at a cottage near, thinking that it would afford some protection, and brought it to his charge. The king folded it up to make a cushion to sit upon; for, worn out as he was with hard fighting all the day before, and hard riding all the night, he could not stand; so he chose to use his blanket as a protection from the wet ground beneath him, and to take the rain upon his head as it fell.

Richard sent a peasant's wife to him presently with some food. Charles, who never had any great respect for the female sex, was alarmed to find that a woman had been entrusted with such a secret.

"My good woman," said he, "can you be faithful to a distressed Cavalier?"

"Yes, sir," said she; "I will die rather than betray you."

Charles had, in fact, no occasion to fear. Woman is, indeed, communicative and confiding, and often, in unguarded hours, reveals indiscreetly what it would have been better to have withheld; but in all cases where real and important trusts are committed to her keeping, there is no human fidelity which can be more safely relied upon than hers.

Charles remained in the wood all the day, exposed to the pelting of the storm. There was a road in sight, a sort of by-way leading across the country, and the monarch beguiled the weary hours as well as he could by watching this road from under the trees, to see if any soldiers came along. There was one troop that appeared, but it passed directly by, marching heavily through the mud and rain, the men intent, apparently, only on reaching their journey's end. When night came on, Richard Penderel returned, approaching cautiously, and, finding all safe, took the king into the house with him. They brought him to the fire, changed and dried his clothes, and gave him supper. The homeless monarch once more enjoyed the luxuries of warmth and shelter.

During all the day, while he had been alone in the wood, he had been revolving in his mind the strange circumstances of his situation, vainly endeavoring, for many hours, to realize what seemed at first like a dreadful dream. Could it be really true that he, the monarch of three kingdoms, so recently at the head of a victorious army, and surrounded by generals and officers of state, was now a friendless and solitary fugitive, without even a place to hide his head from the cold autumnal storm? It seemed at first a dream; but it soon became a reality, and he began to ponder, in every form, the question what he should do. He looked east, west, north, and south, but could not see, in any quarter, any hope of succor, or any reasonable prospect of escape. He, however, arrived at the conclusion, before night came on, that it would be, on the whole, the best plan for him to attempt to escape into Wales.

He was very near the frontier of that country. There was no difficulty to be apprehended on the road thither, excepting in the crossing of the Severn, which, as has already been remarked, flows from north to south not far from the line of the frontier. He thought, too, that if he could once succeed in getting into Wales, he could find secure retreats among the mountains there until he should be able to make his way to some sea-port on the coast trading with France, and so find his way back across the Channel. He proposed this plan to Richard in the evening, and asked him to accompany him as his guide. Richard readily consented, and the arrangements for the journey were made. They adjusted the king's dress again to complete his disguise, and Richard gave him a bill-hook—a sort of woodman's tool—to carry in his hand. It was agreed, also, that his name should be Will Jones so far as there should be any necessity for designating him by a name in the progress of the journey.

They set out at nine o'clock that same night, in the darkness and rain. They wished to get to Madely, a town near the river, before the morning. Richard knew a Mr. Woolf there, a friend of the Royalist cause, who he thought would shelter them, and aid them in getting across the river. They went on very well for some time, until they came to a stream, a branch of the Severn, where there was a bridge, and on the other side a mill. The miller happened to be watching that night at his door. At such times everybody is on the alert, suspecting mischief or danger in every unusual sight or sound.

Hearing the footsteps, he called out, "Who goes there?"

"Neighbors," replied Richard. The king was silent. He had been previously charged by Richard not to speak, except when it could not possibly be avoided, as he had not the accent of the country. "Stop, then," said the miller, "if you be neighbors." The travelers only pressed forward the faster for this challenge. "Stop!" repeated the miller, "if you be neighbors, or I will knock you down;" and he ran out in pursuit of them, armed apparently with the means of executing his threat. Richard fled, the king closely following him. They turned into a lane, and ran a long distance, the way being in many places so dark that the king, in following Richard, was guided only by the sound of his footsteps, and the creaking of the leather dress which such peasants were accustomed in those days to wear. They crept along, however, as silently, and yet as rapidly as possible, until at length Richard turned suddenly aside, leaped over a sort of gap in the hedge, and crouched down in the trench on the other side. Here they remained for some time, listening to ascertain whether they were pursued. When they found that all was still, they crept forth from their hiding places, regained the road, and went on their way.

At length they arrived at the town. Richard left the king concealed in an obscure corner of the street, while he went to the house of Mr. Woolf to see if he could obtain admission. All was dark and still. He knocked till he had aroused some of the family, and finally brought Mr. Woolf to the door.

He told Mr. Woolf that he came to ask shelter for a gentleman who was wishing to get into Wales, and who could not safely travel by day. Mr. Woolf hesitated, and began to ask for further information in respect to the stranger. Richard said that he was an officer who had made his escape from the battle of Worcester, "Then," said Mr. Woolf, "I should hazard my life by concealing him, which I should not be willing to do for any body, unless it were the king." Richard then told him that it *was* his majesty. On hearing this, Mr. Woolf decided at once to admit and conceal the travelers, and Richard went back to bring the king.

When they arrived at the house, they found Mr. Woolf making preparations for their reception. They placed the king by the fire to warm and dry his clothes, and they gave him such food as could be provided on so sudden an emergency. As the morning was now approaching, it was necessary to adopt some plan of concealment for the day, and Mr. Woolf decided upon concealing his guests in his barn. He said that there were holes and hiding places built in his house, but that they had all been discovered on some previous search, and, in case of any suspicion or alarm, the officers would go directly to them all. He took the travelers, accordingly, to the barn, and concealed them there among the hay. He said that he would himself, during the day, make inquiries in respect to the practicability of their going on upon their journey, and come and report to them in the evening.

Accordingly, when the evening came, Mr. Woolf returned, relieved them from their confinement, and took them back again to the house. His report, however, in respect to the continuance of their journey, was very unfavorable. He thought it would be impossible, he said, for them to cross the Severn. The Republican forces had stationed guards at all the bridges, ferries, and fords, and at every other practicable place of crossing, and no one was allowed to pass without a strict examination. The country was greatly excited, too, with the intelligence of the king's escape; rewards were offered for his apprehension, and heavy penalties denounced upon all who should harbor or conceal him. Under these circumstances, Mr. Woolf recommended that Charles should go back to Boscobel, and conceal himself as securely as possible there, until some plan could be devised for effecting his escape from the country.

The king had no alternative but to accede to this plan. He waited at Mr. Woolf's house till midnight, in order that the movement in the streets of the town might have time entirely to subside, and then, disappointed and discouraged by the failure of his hopes, he prepared to set out upon his return. Mr. Woolf made some changes in his disguise, and bathed his face in a decoction of walnut leaves, which he had prepared during the day, to alter his complexion, which was naturally very dark and peculiar, and thus exposed him to danger of discovery. When all was ready, the two travelers bade their kind host farewell, and crept forth again through the silent streets, to return, by the way they came, back to Boscobel.

They went on very well till they began to approach the branch stream where they had met with their adventure with the miller. They could not cross this stream by the bridge without going by the mill again, which they were both afraid to do. The king proposed that they should go a little way below, and ford the stream. Richard was afraid to attempt this, as he could not swim; and as the night was dark, and the current rapid, there would be imminent danger of their getting beyond their depth. Charles said that *he* could swim, and that he would, accordingly, go first and try the water. They groped their way down, therefore, to the bank, and Charles, leaving his guide upon the land, waded in, and soon disappeared from view as he receded from the shore. He returned, however, after a short time, in safety, and reported the passage practicable, as the water was only three or four feet deep; so, taking Richard by the hand, he led him into the stream. It was a dismal and dangerous undertaking, wading thus through a deep and rapid current in darkness and cold, but they succeeded in passing safely over.

They reached Boscobel before the morning dawned, and Richard, when they arrived, left the king in the wood while he went toward the house to reconnoiter, and see if all was safe. He found within an officer of the king's army, a certain Colonel Carlis, who had fled from Worcester some time after the king had left the field, and, being acquainted with the situation of Boscobel, had sought refuge there; William Penderel, who had remained in charge of Boscobel, having received and secreted him when he arrived.

Richard and William brought Colonel Carlis out into the wood to see the king. They found him sitting upon the ground at the foot of a tree, entirely exhausted. He was worn out with hardship and fatigue. They took him to the house. They brought him to the fire, and gave him some food. The colonel drew off his majesty's heavy peasant shoes and coarse stockings. They were soaked with water and full of gravel. The colonel bathed his feet, which were sadly swollen and blistered, and, as there were no other shoes in the house which would answer for him to wear, Dame Penderel warmed and dried those which the colonel had taken off, by filling them with hot ashes from the fire, and then put them on again.

The king continued to enjoy such sort of comforts as these during the night, but when the morning drew near it became necessary to look out for some place of concealment. The Penderels thought that no place within the house would be safe, for there was danger every hour of the arrival of a band of soldiers, who would not fail to search the mansion most effectually in every part. There was the wood near by, which was very secluded and solitary; but still they feared that, in case of a search, the wood would be explored as effectually as the dwelling. Under these circumstances, Carlis was looking around, perplexed and uncertain, not knowing what to do, when he perceived some scattered oaks standing by themselves in a field not far from the house, one of which seemed to be so full and dense in its foliage as to afford some hope of concealment there. The tree, it seems, had been headed down once or twice, and this pruning had had the effect, usual in such cases, of making the branches spread and grow very thick and full. The colonel thought that though, in making a search for fugitives, men might very naturally explore a thicket or a grove, they would not probably think of examining a detached and solitary tree; he proposed, accordingly, that the king and himself should climb up into this spreading oak, and conceal themselves for the day among its branches.

The king consented to this plan. They took some provisions, therefore, as soon as the day began to dawn, and something to answer the purpose of a cushion, and proceeded to the tree. By the help of William and Richard the king and the colonel climbed up, and established themselves in the top. The colonel placed the cushion for the king on the best support among the limbs that he could find. The bread and cheese, and a small bottle of beer, which Richard and William had brought for their day's supplies, they suspended to a branch within their reach. The colonel then seated himself a little above the king, in such a manner that the monarch's head could rest conveniently in his lap, and in as easy a position as it was possible, under such circumstances, to attain. Richard and William, then, after surveying the place of retreat all around from below, in order to be sure that the concealment afforded by the foliage was every where complete, went away, promising to keep faithful watch during the day and to return in the evening. All things being thus arranged in the oak, the colonel bade his majesty to close his eyes and go to sleep, saying that he would take good care that he did not fall. The king followed his directions, and slept safely for many hours.

In the course of the day the king and Carlis saw, by means of the openings between the leaves, through which, as through loop holes in a tower, they continually reconnoitered the surrounding fields, men passing to and fro, some of whom they imagined to be soldiers searching the wood. They were not, however, themselves molested. They passed the day undisturbed, except by the incessant anxiety and alarm which they necessarily suffered, and the fatigue and pain, which must have become almost intolerable before night, from their constrained and comfórtless position. Night, however, came at last, and relieved them from their duress. They descended from the tree and stole back cautiously to the house, the king resolving that he could not bear such hardship another day, and that they must, accordingly, find some other hiding place for him on the morrow. We can scarcely be surprised at this decision. A wild beast could hardly have endured a second day in such a lair.

Other plans of concealment for the king were accordingly formed that night, and measures were soon concerted, as we shall see in the next chapter, to effect his escape from the country. The old tree, however, which had sheltered him so safely, was not forgotten. In after years, when the monarch was restored to his throne, and the story of his dangers and his escape was made known throughout the kingdom, thousands of visitors came to look upon the faithful tree which had thus afforded his majesty its unconscious but effectual protection. Every one took away a leaf or a sprig for a souvenir, and when, at last, the proprietor found that there was danger that the whole tree would be carried away unless he interposed, he fenced it in and tilled the ground around it, to defend it from further mutilation. It has borne the name of the Royal Oak from that time to the present day, and has been the theme of narrators and poets without number, who have celebrated its praises in every conceivable form of composition. There is, however, probably no one of them all who has done more for the wide extension of its fame among all the ranks and gradations of society than the unknown author of the humble distich,

> "*The royal oak, it was the tree,*
> *That saved his royal majesty.*"

VIII

THE KING'S ESCAPE TO FRANCE

WHEN the king and Carlis came into the house again, on the evening after their wearisome day's confinement in the tree, Dame Penderel had some chickens prepared for his majesty's supper, which he enjoyed as a great and unexpected luxury. They showed him, too, the hiding hole, built in the walls, where the Earl of Derby had been concealed, and where they proposed that he should be lodged for the night. There was room in it to lay down a small straw pallet for a bed. The king thought it would be very secure, and was confirmed in his determination not to go again to the oak. Before his majesty retired, Carlis asked him what he would like to have to eat on the morrow. He said that he should like some mutton. Carlis assented, and, bidding his master good night, he left him to his repose.

There was no mutton in the house, and Richard and William both agreed that it would be unsafe for either of them to procure any, since, as they were not accustomed to purchase such food, their doing so now would awaken suspicion that they had some unusual guest to provide for. The colonel, accordingly, undertook himself to obtain the supply.

Getting the necessary directions, therefore, from Richard and William, he went to the house of a farmer at some little distance—a tenant, he was, on the Boscobel estate—and groped his way to the sheep-cote. He selected an animal, such as he thought suitable for his purpose, and butchered it with his dagger. He then went back to the house, and sent William Penderel to bring the plunder home.

William dressed a leg of the mutton, and sent it in the morning into the room which they had assigned to the king, near his hiding hole. The king was overjoyed at the prospect of this feast He called for a carving knife and a frying pan. He cut off some callops from the joint, and then, after frying the meat with Carlis's assistance, they ate it together.

The king, becoming now somewhat accustomed to his situation, began to grow a little more bold. He walked in a little gallery which opened from his room. There was a window in this gallery which commanded a view of the road. The king kept watch carefully at this window as he walked to and fro, that he might observe the first appearance of any enemy's approach. It was observed, too, that he apparently spent some time here in exercises of devotion, imploring, probably, the protection of Heaven, in this his hour of danger and distress. The vows and promises which he doubtless made were, however, all forgotten, as usual in such cases, when safety and prosperity came again.

There was a little garden, too, near the house, with an eminence at the further end of it, where there was an arbor, with a stone table, and seats about it. It was retired, and yet, being in an elevated position, it answered, like the window of the gallery in the house, the double purpose of a hiding place and a watch tower. It was far more comfortable, and probably much more safe, than the wretched nest in the tree of the day before; for, were the king discovered in the arbor, there would be some chances of escape from detection still remaining, but to have been found in the tree would have been certain destruction.

In the mean time, the Penderels had had messengers out during the Saturday and Sunday, communicating with certain known friends of the king in the neighboring towns, and endeavoring to concert some plan for his escape. They were successful in these consultations, and be fore Sunday night a plan was formed. It seems there was a certain Colonel Lane, whose wife had obtained a pass from the authorities of the Republican army to go to Bristol, on the occasion of the sickness of a relative, and to take with her a man servant. Bristol was a hundred miles to the southward, near the mouth of the Severn. It was thought that if the king should reach this place, he could, perhaps, succeed afterward in making his way to the southern coast of England, and embarking there, at some sea-port, for France. The plan was accordingly formed for Mrs. Lane to go, as she had designed, on this journey, and to take the king along with her in the guise of her servant. The arrangements were all made, and the king was to be met in a wood five or six miles from Boscobel, early on Monday morning, by some trusty friends, who were afterward to conceal him for a time in their houses, until all things should be ready for the journey.

The king found, however, when the morning approached, that his feet were in such a condition that he could not walk. They accordingly procured a horse belonging to one of the Penderels, and put him upon it. The brothers all accompanied him as he went away. They were armed with concealed weapons, intending, if they we're attacked by any small party, to defend the king with their lives. They, however, went on without any molestation. It was a dark and rainy night. Nights are seldom otherwise in England in September. The brothers Penderel, six of them in all, guided the king along through the darkness and rain, until they were within a mile or two of the appointed place of meeting, where the king dismounted, for the purpose of walking the rest of way, for greater safety, and three of the brothers, taking the horse with them, returned. The rest went on, and, after delivering the king safely into the hands of his friends, who were waiting at the appointed place to receive him, bade his majesty farewell, and, expressing their good wishes for the safe accomplishment of his escape, they returned to Boscobel.

They now altered the king's disguise in some degree, to accommodate the change in his assumed character from that of a peasant of the woods to a respectable farmer's son, such as would be a suitable traveling attendant for an English dame, and they gave him the new name of William Jackson in the place of Will Jones. Mrs. Lane's sister's husband was to go with them a part of the way, and there was another gentleman and lady also of the party, so they were five in all. The horses were brought to the door when all was ready, just in the edge of the evening, the pretended attendant standing respectfully by, with his hat under his arm. He was to ride upon the same horse with Mrs. Lane, the lady being seated on a pillion behind him. The family assembled to bid the party farewell, none, either of the travelers or of the spectators, except Mrs. Lane and her brother-in-law, having any idea that the meek looking William Jackson was any other than what he seemed.

They traveled on day after day, meeting with various adventures, and apparently with narrow escapes. At one time a shoe was off from the horse's foot, and the king stopped at a blacksmith's to have it replaced. While the smith was busy at the work, the king, standing by, asked him what news. "No news," said the smith, "that I know of, since the grand news of beating the rogues, the Scots, at Worcester." The king asked if any of the English officers who were with the Scots had been taken since the battle. "Some had been captured," the smith replied, "but he could not learn that the rogue Charles Stuart had been taken." The king then told him that if that rogue were taken, he deserved to be hanged more than all the rest, for bringing the Scots in. "You speak like an honest man," said the smith. Soon after, the work was done, and Charles led the horse away.

At another time, when the party had stopped for the night, the king, in accordance with his assumed character, went to the kitchen. They were roasting some meat with a jack, a machine used much in those days to keep meat, while roasting, in slow rotation before the fire, The jack had run down. They asked the pretended William Jackson to wind it up. In trying to do it, he attempted to wind it the wrong way. The cook, in ridiculing, his awkwardness, asked him what country he came from, that he did not know how to wind up a jack. The king meekly replied that he was the son of a poor tenant of Colonel Lane's, and that they seldom had meat to roast at home, and that, when they had it, they did not roast it with a jack. The party at length arrived safely at their place of destination, which was at the house of a Mrs. Norton, at a place called Leigh, about three miles from Bristol. Here the whole party were received, and, in order to seclude the king as much as possible from observation, Mrs. Lane pretended that he was in very feeble health, and he was, accordingly, a good deal confined to his room. The disease which they selected for him was an intermittent fever, which came on only at intervals. This would account for his being sometimes apparently pretty well, and allowed him occasionally, when tired of being shut up in his room, to come down and join the other servants, and hear their conversation.

There was an old servant of the family, named Pope, a butler, to whose care the pretended William Jackson was specially confided. On the following morning after his arrival, Charles, feeling, notwithstanding his fever, a good appetite after the fatigues of his journey, went down to get his breakfast, and, while there, some men came in, friends of the servants, and Pope brought out a luncheon of bread and ale, and placed it before them. While they were eating it, they began to talk about the battle of Worcester, and one of the men described it so accurately, that the king perceived that he must have been there. On questioning him more particularly, the man said that he was a soldier in the king's army, and he began to describe the person and appearance of the king. Charles was alarmed, and very soon rose and went away. Pope, who had had, it seems, his suspicions before, was now confirmed in them. He went to Mrs. Lane, and told her that he knew very well that their stranger guest was the king. She denied most positively that it was so, but she immediately took measures to communicate the conversation to Charles. The result of their consultations, and of their inquiries about the character of Pope for prudence and fidelity, was to admit him to their confidence, and endeavor to secure his aid. He was faithful in keeping the secret, and he rendered the king afterward a great deal of very efficient aid.

There was a certain Colonel Wyndham, whose name has become immortalized by his connection with the king's escape, who lived at a place called Trent, not far from the southern coast of England. After much deliberation and many inquiries, it was decided that the king should proceed there while arrangements should be made for his embarkation. When this plan was formed, Mrs. Lane received a pretended letter from home, saying that her father was taken suddenly and dangerously sick, and urging her immediate return. They set out accordingly, William having so far recovered from his fever as to be able to travel again!

During all this time, Lord Wilmot, who has already been mentioned as a fellow fugitive with Charles from the battle of Worcester, had followed the party of the king in his progress through the country, under various disguises, and by different modes of travel, keeping near his royal master all the way, and obtaining stolen interviews with him, from time to time, for consultation. In this way each rendered the other very essential aid. The two friends arrived at last at Colonel Wyndham's together. Mrs. Lane and her party here took leave of the king, and returned northward toward her home.

Colonel Wyndham was a personal acquaintance of the king. He had been an officer under Charles I., in the civil wars preceding that monarch's captivity and death, and Charles, who, as Prince of Wales, had made a campaign as will be recollected, in the west of England before he went to France, had had frequent intercourse with Wyndham, and bad great confidence in his fidelity. The colonel had been at last shut up in a castle, and had finally surrendered on such conditions as secured his own liberty and safety. He had, consequently, since been allowed to live quietly at his own estate in Trent, though he was watched and suspected by the government as a known friend of the king's. Charles had, of course, great confidence in him. He was very cordially received into his house, and very securely secreted there.

It would be dangerous for Wyndham himself to do any thing openly in respect to finding a vessel to convey the king to France. He accordingly engaged a trusty friend to go down to the sea-port on the coast which was nearest to his residence, and see what he could do. This sea-port was Lyme, or Lyme-Regis, as it is sometimes called. It was about twenty-five miles from Trent, where Wyndham resided, toward the southwest, and about the same distance to the eastward of Exeter, where Charles's mother had some years before sought refuge from her husband's enemies.

Colonel Wyndham's messenger went to Lyme. He found there, pretty soon, the master of a small vessel, which was accustomed to ply back and forth to one of the ports on the coast of France, to carry merchandise. The messenger, after making inquiries, and finding that the captain, if captain he may be called, was the right sort of man for such an enterprise, obtained an interview with him and introduced conversation by asking when he expected to go back to France. The captain replied that it would probably be some time before he should be able to make up another cargo. "How should you like to take some passengers?" said the messenger. "Passengers?" inquired the captain. "Yes," rejoined the other; "there are two gentlemen here who wish to cross the Channel privately, and they are willing to pay fifty pounds to be landed at any port on the other side. Will you take them?"

The captain perceived that it was a serious business. There was a proclamation out, offering a reward for the apprehension of the king, or Charles Stuart as they called him, and also for other of the leaders at the battle of Worcester. All persons, too, were strictly prohibited from taking any one across the Channel; and to conceal the king, or to connive in any way at his escape, was death. The captain, however, at length agreed to the proposal, influenced as the colonel's messenger supposed, partly by the amount of his pay, and partly by his interest in the Royal cause. He agreed to make his little vessel ready without delay.

They did not think it prudent for the king to attempt to embark at Lyme, but there was, a few miles to the eastward of it, along the shore, a small village named Charmouth, where there was a creek jutting up from the sea, and a little pier, sufficient for the landing of so small a vessel as the one they had engaged. It was agreed that, on an appointed day, the king and Lord Wilmot were to come down to Charmouth, and take up their lodgings at the inn; that in the night the captain was to sail out of the port of Lyme, in the most private manner possible, and come to Charmouth; and that the king and Wilmot, who would, in the mean time, be watching from the inn, when they saw the light of the approaching vessel, should come down to the pier and embark, and the captain then immediately sail away.

The messenger accordingly went back to Colonel Wyndham's with intelligence of the plan that he had formed, while the captain of the vessel went to work as privately as possible to lay in his stores and make his other preparations for sea. He did this with the utmost precaution and secrecy, and succeeded in deceiving every body but his wife. Wives have the opportunity to perceive indications of the concealed existence of matters of moment and weight which others do not enjoy, in studying the countenances of their husbands. A man can easily, through the day, when surrounded by the world, assume an unconcerned and careless air, though oppressed with a very considerable mental burden; but when he comes home at night, he instinctively throws off half his disguise, and conjugal watchfulness and solicitude easily penetrate the remainder. At least it was so in this case. The captain's dame perceived that her husband was thoughtful and absent minded. She watched him. She observed some indications that he was making preparations for sea. She asked him what it meant. He said he did not know how soon he might have a cargo, and he wanted to be all ready in season. His wife, however, was not satisfied. She watched him more closely still, and when the appointed night came on which he had agreed to sail, finding that it was impossible for him to elude her vigilance, he told her plainly, that he was going across the Channel on private business, but that he should immediately return.

She declared positively that he should not go. She knew, she said, that the business was something which would end in ruining him and his family, and she was determined that he should not risk her safety and his own life in any such desperate and treasonable plans. She locked the door upon him, and when he insisted on being released, she declared that if he did attempt to go, she would immediately give warning to the authorities, and have him arrested and confined. So the discomfited captain was compelled to give up his design, and break his appointment at the Charmouth pier.

In the mean time, the king and Lord Wilmot came down, as had been agreed upon, to Charmouth, and put up, with many other travelers, at the inn. There was great excitement all over that part of the country, every one talking about the battle of Worcester, the escape of the king, and especially about an expedition which Cromwell had been organizing, which was then assembling on the southern coast. Its destination was the island of Jersey, which had thus far adhered to the Royalist cause, and which Cromwell was now intending to reduce to subjection to him. The bustle and movement which all these causes combined to create, made the king and Lord Wilmot very anxious and uneasy. There were assemblies convened in the villages which they passed through, and men were haranguing the populace on the victories which had been gained, and on the future measures to be pursued. In one place the bells were ringing, and bonfires were burning in celebration of the death of the king, it being rumored and believed that he had been shot.

Our two fugitives, however, arrived safely at the inn, put up their horses, and began to watch anxiously for the light of the approaching vessel. They watched, of course, in vain. Midnight came, but no vessel. They waited hour after hour, till at last morning dawned, and they found that all hope of accomplishing their enterprise must be abandoned. They could not remain where they were, however, another day, without suspicion; so they prepared to move on and seek temporary refuge in some other neighboring town, while they could send one of the attendants who came with them back to Colonel Wyndham's, to see if he could ascertain the cause of the failure. One or two days were spent in inquiries, negotiations, and delays. The result was, that all hope of embarking at Lyme had to be abandoned, and it was concluded that the fugitives should proceed on to the eastward, along the coast, to the care of another Royalist, a certain Colonel Gunter, who might perhaps find means to send them away from some port in that part of the country. At any rate, they would, by this plan, escape the excitements and dangers which seemed to environ them in the neighborhood of Lyme.

It was fortunate that they went away from Charmouth when they did; by doing so they narrowly escaped apprehension; for that night, while the king's horse was in the stable, a smith was sent for to set a shoe upon the horse of one of the other travelers. After finishing his work, he began to examine the feet of the other horses in the stalls, and when he came to the one which the king had rode, his attention was particularly attracted to the condition and appearance of the shoes, and he remarked to those who were with him that that horse had come a long journey, and that of the four shoes, he would warrant that no two had been made in the same county. This remark was quoted the next day, and the mysterious circumstance, trifling as it was, was sufficient, in the highly excitable state of the public mind, to awaken attention. People came to see the horse, and to inquire for the owner, but they found that both had disappeared. They immediately determined that the stranger must have been the king, or at least some distinguished personage in disguise, and they sent in search of the party in every direction; but the travelers had taken such effectual precautions to blind all pursuit that their track could not be followed.

In the mean time, the king journeyed secretly on from the residence of one faithful adherent to another, encountering many perplexities, and escaping narrowly many dangers, until he came at last to the neighborhood of Shoreham, a town upon the coast of Sussex. Colonel Gunter had provided a vessel here. It was a small vessel, bound, with a load of coal, along the coast, to the westward, to a port called Pool, beyond the Isle of Wight. Colonel Gunter had arranged it with the master to deviate from his voyage, by crossing over to the coast of France, and leaving his passengers there. He was then to return, and proceed to his original destination. Both the owner of the vessel and the master who commanded it were Royalists, but they had not been told that it was the king whom they were going to convey. In the bargain which had been made with them, the passengers had been designated simply as two gentlemen of rank who had escaped from the battle of Worcester. When, however, the master of the vessel saw the king, he immediately recognized him, having seen him before in his campaigns under his father. This, however, seemed to make no difference in his readiness to convey the passengers away. He said that hews perfectly willing to risk his life to save that of his sovereign, and the arrangements for the embarkation proceeded.

The little vessel—its burden was about sixty tons—was brought into a small cove at Brighthelmstone, a few miles to the eastward from Shoreham, and run upon the beach, where it was left stranded when the tide went down. The king and Lord Wilmot went to it by night, ascended its side by a ladder, went down immediately into the cabin, and concealed themselves there. When the rising tide had lifted the vessel, with its precious burden, gently from the sand, the master made easy sail, and coasted along the English shore toward the Isle of Wight, which was the direction of the voyage which he had originally intended to make. He did not wish the people at Shoreham to observe any alteration of his course, since that might have awakened suspicion, and possibly invited pursuit; so they went on for a time to the westward, which was a course that rather increased than diminished their distance from their place of destination.

It was seven o'clock in the morning when they sailed. There was a gentle October breeze from the north, which carried them slowly along the shore, and in the afternoon the Isle of Wight came fully into view. There were four men and a boy on board the ship, constituting the crew. The master came to the king in the cabin, and proposed to him, as a measure of additional security, and to prevent the possibility of any opposition on the part of the sailors to the proposed change in their course which it would now soon be necessary to make, that the king and Lord Wilmot should propose the plan of going to France to them, asking their interest with the captain in obtaining his consent, as it had not yet been mentioned to the captain at all; for the sailors had of course understood that the voyage was only the usual coastwise trip to the port of Pool, and that these strangers were ordinary travelers, going on that voyage. The master, therefore, thought that there would be less danger of difficulty if the king were first to gain the sailors over himself, by promises or rewards, and then all come together to gain the captain's consent, which could then, at last, with apparent reluctance, be accorded.

This plan was pursued. The two travelers went to the sailors upon the forecastle, and told them, with an air of honest confidence, that they were not what they seemed. They were merchants, they said, and were unfortunately a little in debt, and under the necessity of leaving England for a time. They had some money due to them in Rouen, in France, and they wanted very much to be taken across the Channel to Dieppe, or some port near Rouen. They made known their condition to the sailors, they said, because they wanted their intercession with the captain to take them over, and they gave the sailors a good generous present in money for them to spend in drink; not so generous, however, as to cast suspicion upon their story of being traders in distress.

Sailors are easily persuaded by arguments that are enforced by small presents of money. They consented to the plan, and then the king and Lord Wilmot went to express their wishes to the captain. He made many objections. It would delay him on his voyage, and lead to many inconveniences. The passengers, however, urged their request, the sailors seconding them. The wind was fair, and they could easily run across the Channel, and then, after they landed, the captain could pursue his course to the place of his destination. The captain finally consented; the helm was altered, the sails were trimmed, and the little vessel bore away toward its new destination on the coast of France.

It was now five o'clock in the afternoon. The English coast soon disappeared from the horizon, and the next morning, at daylight, they could see the French shore. They approached the land at a little port called Fecamp. The wind, however, failed them before they got quite to the land, and they had to anchor to wait for a turn of the tide to help them in. In this situation, they were soon very much alarmed by the appearance of a vessel in the offing, which was coming also toward the shore. They thought it was a Spanish privateer, and its appearance brought a double apprehension. There was danger that the privateer would capture them, France and Spain being then at war. There was danger, also, that the master of their vessel, afraid himself of being captured, might insist on making all haste back again to the English coast; for the wind, though contrary so long as they wished to go on into their harbor, was fair for taking them away. The king and Lord Wilmot consulted together, and came to the conclusion to go ashore in the little boat. They soon made a bargain with the sailors to row them, and, hastily descending the vessel's side, they entered the boat, and pushed off over the rolling surges of the Channel.

They were two miles from the shore, but they reached it in safety. The sailors went back to the vessel. The privateer turned out to be a harmless trader coming into port. The English vessel recrossed the Channel, and went on to its original port of destination; and Lord Wilmot and the king, relieved now of all their anxieties and fears, walked in their strange English dress up into the village to the inn.

IX

THE RESTORATION

As the readers of a tale are generally inclined to sympathize with the hero of it, both in his joys and in his sorrows, whether he is deserving of sympathy or not, they who follow the adventures of Charles in his wanderings in England after the unfortunate battle of Worcester, feel ordinarily quite a strong sensation of pleasure at finding him at last safely landed on the French shore. Charles himself doubtless experienced at first an overwhelming emotion of exultation and joy at having thus saved himself from the desperate dangers of his condition in England. On cool reflection, however, he soon perceived that there was but little cause for rejoicing in his condition and prospects. There were dangers and sufferings enough still before him, different, it is true, from those in which he had been involved, but still very dark and threatening in character. He had now, in fact, ten years of privation, poverty, and exile before him, full of troubles from beginning to end.

The new series of troubles began to come upon him, too, very soon. When he and his companion went up to the inn, on the morning of their landing, dressed as they were in the guise of Englishmen of humble rank, and having been put ashore, too, from a vessel which immediately afterward sailed away, they were taken for English thieves, or fugitives from justice, and refused admission to the inn. They sent to some gentlemen of the neighborhood, to whom they made themselves known, so that this difficulty was removed, their urgent wants were supplied, and they were provided with the means of transportation to Paris. Of course, the mother of the fugitive monarch, yet almost a boy, was rejoiced to welcome him, but he received no very cordial welcome from any one else. Now that Charles had finally abandoned England, his adherents there gave up his cause, of course, as totally lost. The Republicans, with Cromwell at their head, established a very firm and efficient government, which the nations of the Continent soon began to find that it would be incumbent on them to respect. For any foreign court to harbor a pretender to the British crown, when there was an established government in England based on a determination of the people to abrogate royalty altogether, was to incur very considerable political danger. Charles soon found that, under these circumstances, he was not likely to be long a very welcome guest in the French palaces.

He remained, however, in Paris for a short time, endeavoring to find some way to retrieve his ruined fortunes. Anne Maria was still there, and he attempted to renew his suit to her. She listened to the entertaining stories which he told of his dangers and escapes in England, and for a time, as Charles thought, encouraged his attentions. In fact, at one time he really believed that the affair was all settled, and began to assume that it was so in speaking with her upon the subject. She, however, at length undeceived him, in a conversation which ended with her saying that she thought he had better go back to England, and "either get his head broken, or else have a crown upon it." The fact was, that Anne Maria was now full of a new scheme for being married to Louis XIV. himself, who, though much younger than she, had attained now to a marriageable age, and she had no intention of regarding Charles in any other light than as one of the ordinary crowd of her admirers. She finally extinguished all his hopes by coolly requesting him not to visit her so frequently.

In addition to his other sources of discomfort. Charles disagreed with his mother. She was a very decided Catholic, and he a Protestant, from policy it is true, and not principle, but he was none the less rigid and inflexible on that account. He and his mother disagreed in respect to the education of the younger children. They were both restricted in their means, too, and subject to a thousand mortifications from this cause, in the proud and haughty circle in which they moved. Finally, the king decided to leave Paris altogether, and try to find a more comfortable refuge in Holland.

His sister and her husband, the Prince of Orange, had always treated him, as well as all the rest of the family, with great kindness and attention; but now, to complete the catalogue of his disasters, the Prince of Orange died, the power of the government passed into other hands, and Mary found herself deprived of influence and honor, and reduced all at once to a private station. She would have been glad to continue her protection to her brother, but the new government feared the power of Cromwell. Cromwell sent word to them that England would consider their harboring of the fugitive as tantamount to a declaration of war; so they notified Charles that he must leave their dominions, and find, if he could, some other place of retreat. He went up the Rhine to the city of Cologne, where it is said he found a widow woman, who received him as a lodger without pay, trusting to his promise to recompense her at some future time. There is generally little risk in giving credit to European monarchs, expelled by the temporary triumph of Republicanism from their native realms. They are generally pretty certain of being sooner or later restored to their thrones.

At any rate, Charles was restored, and his restoration was effected in a manner wholly unexpected to all mankind. In order that the circumstances may be clearly understood, the reader must recall it to mind that Charles the First had been deposed and beheaded by the action of a Parliament, and that this Parliament was, of course, at his death the depository of sovereign power in England. In a short time, however, the army, with Cromwell at its head, became too strong for the Parliament. Cromwell assumed the supreme power under the name of the Protector. He dissolved Parliament, and expelled the members from their seats. He governed the country as protector for many years, and when at length he died, his son Richard Cromwell attempted to take his place. Richard did not, however, possess the talent and energy of his father, and he soon found himself totally inadequate to manage the affairs of government in such stormy times. He was deposed, and the old Parliament which Cromwell had broken up was restored.

There followed, then, a new contest between the Parliament and the army, with an officer named Lambert at the head of the latter. The army proved the strongest. Lambert stationed guards in the streets leading to the Parliament House one day when the members were about to assemble, and turned the members all back as they came. When the speaker arrived in his carriage, he ordered his soldiers to take hold of the horses' heads and turn them round, and lead them home again. Thus there was no actual outward violence, but the members of Parliament were intimidated, and gave up the attempt to exercise their power, though they still reserved their claim, and their party was busy all over the kingdom in attempting to restore them to their functions. In the mean time, the army appointed a sort of council, which they invested with supreme authority.

It does not come within the scope and design of this volume to give a full account of the state of public affairs during the interregnum between the death of Charles I. and the Restoration of the monarchy under Charles II., nor of the points of controversy at issue among the various parties formed. The reader, however, must not suppose that, during this period, there was at any time what could, with any propriety, be called a republic. A true republic exists only where the questions of government are fairly and honorably submitted to the whole population, with a universal disposition to acquiesce peaceably in the decision of the majority, when that is ascertained. There probably has never been any such state of things as this in any country of Europe since the Christian era. There certainly was no such state of things in England in the time of the Commonwealth. There were a great many persons who wished to have it so, and who called themselves Republicans; but their plan, if that were indeed their plan, was never tried. Very likely it was not practicable to try it. At any rate, it certainly was not tried. The sovereignty taken from the Stuart dynasty in the person of Charles I. *was never vested in the people at large*. It was seized forcibly by the various powers already existing in the state, as they found themselves, one after another, able to seize it. The Parliament took, it from Charles. The army took it from Parliament. Then Oliver Cromwell took it from the army. He found himself strong enough to hold it as long as he lived, and when he died he delivered it to his son Richard. Richard could not hold it. The Parliament rose to a sort of supplementary existence, and took it from Richard, and then the army took it from Parliament again. Finally, General Monk appeared upon the stage in Scotland, as we shall presently see, marched down through England, and, with the help of thousands and thousands who were tired of these endless changes, took it from the army and restored it once more to the Parliament, on condition of their placing it back again in the hands of the king. Thus there was no republic at all, from beginning to end.

Nor is it at all certain that there ought to have been. The difficulties of really, truly, and honestly laying the national sovereignty in the hands of the whole population of such a realm as England, and of so organizing the population that its decisions shall actually control the legislation of the country and the public administration of its affairs, are all but insuperable. The English people found the tyranny and oppression of royalty intolerable. They arose and set royalty aside. It devolved, then, on the next strongest power in the state to assume the authority thus divested; this was the Parliament, who governed, just as the king had done, by the exercise of their own superior power, keeping the mass of the community just where they were before. It is true that many individuals of very low rank rose to positions of great power; but they represented only a party, and the power they wielded was monarchical power usurped, not Republican power fairly conferred upon them. Thus, though in the time of the Commonwealth there were plenty of Republicans, there was never a republic. It has always been so in all European revolutions. In America, Legislatures and executive officers of state are only *agents*, through whom the great population itself quietly executes its will, the two millions of votes in the great elections being the real power by which every thing is controlled. But Cromwell, Napoleon, Lamartine, Cavaignac, and all the others, whatever formalities of voting may have attended their induction into office, have always really held their power by force of bayonets, not of ballots. There is great danger that it will continue so in Europe for a long time to come.

But to return. It was in 1659 when the army, with Lambert at its head, expelled the Parliament. All England was now divided into parties, some for the Parliament, some for the army, some for the king. There was a distinguished general in Scotland at this time named Monk. He had been left there by Cromwell in command of the military forces in that country. He was a man considerably advanced in life, and of great circumspection, prudence, and steadiness of character. All parties wished to gain his influence, but he kept his own counsel, and declared openly for neither.

He, however, began to get together his forces, and to make preparations to march into England. People asked him what he intended to do, but he would give no definite answer. He was six weeks getting ready for his expedition, during which time many deputations were sent to him from the various parties, making different propositions to him, each party being eager to obtain his adhesion to their cause. He received all their deputations, heard what they had to say, made no definite reply to any of them, but went on quietly with his work. He got the various divisions of his army at length together, made provisional arrangements for the government of Scotland during his absence, and set out on his march.

He entered England in January, 1660, and advanced toward London. The English army was scattered all over the kingdom; but Monk opened negotiations with the leaders of it, and also with the members of Parliament, and, without committing himself absolutely to either party, he managed to have the Parliament restored. They assembled peaceably in London, and resumed their functions. A part of the English army was there for their protection. Monk, as he approached London, sent word to Parliament asking that quarters might be provided for him and his army there. Parliament, desirous of conciliating him and securing his co-operation in sustaining their power, acceded to this request. The other troops were removed; Monk entered London in triumph, and took possession of all the strong holds there, holding them nominally under Parliamentary authority Monk still kept his ultimate designs profoundly secret. No party very strongly opposed him, for no party knew whether to regard him as an enemy or a friend. The Royalists, however, all over the kingdom, took new courage, and a general expectation began to pervade the minds of men that the monarchy was to be restored. The Parliament rescinded the votes which had been most decisive against the house of Stuart and monarchical rule. The most prominent Republicans were dismissed from office under various pretexts, and men known to be loyal were appointed in their place. Finally, the Parliament itself was dissolved, and writs were issued for the election of a new one, more in accordance with the ancient forms.

When at length this new Parliament assembled, the public mind was in a great fever of excitement, there being a vague expectation every where that the monarchy was to be restored, while yet the Restoration was openly spoken of by no one. The first votes which were taken in the House of Commons indicated a very favorable state of feeling toward monarchy; and at length, a few days after the opening of the session, it was announced that there was a messenger at the door with a communication from the king. The announcement was received with the wildest acclamations of joy. The messenger was immediately ordered to enter. The communication was read, the vast assembly listening with breathless attention.

It contained, in the first place, a letter, in which the king stated that, having heard that the people of England had restored the Parliament according to the ancient forms, he hoped that now the Parliament would go on and complete the good work which had been begun, and heal the distractions of the kingdom by reinstating him as sovereign in the ancient rights and prerogatives of the crown.

The second part of the king's communication, and by far the most important part, was what was called his Declaration, a document in which he announced formally what his intentions were in case he were restored to the throne. One of these assurances was, that he was ready to forgive and forget the past, so far as he might himself be supposed to have cause of complaint against any of his subjects for the part they had taken in the late transactions. He professed his readiness to grant a free pardon to all, excepting those who should be expressly excluded from such pardon by the Parliament itself. The Declaration also set forth that, inasmuch as there was prevailing throughout the country a great diversity of religious opinion, the king, if restored to his throne, whatever his own religious views or those of his government might be, would agree that his subjects should be allowed full liberty of conscience in all respects, and that nobody should be molested in any way on account of his religious faith or usages of worship.

And, finally, the Declaration contained a covenant on the part of the king, that whereas there had been great changes of property, arising from fines and confiscations for political offenses during the period of the Revolution, he would not himself disturb the existing titles to property, but would leave them to be settled on such principles and in such a way as Parliament should direct.

The letter from the king, and especially the Declaration, gave the utmost satisfaction. The latter disarmed those who would otherwise have opposed the return of the king, by quieting their fears of being disturbed in respect to their liberty or their property. Immediately after these papers were read, they were ordered to be published, and were sent every where throughout the kingdom, awakening, wherever they went the greatest demonstrations of joy. The Parliament passed a vote that the ancient Constitution of the kingdom, of government by king, Lords, and Commons, ought to be restored, and they went forth in a body into the public places of the city to proclaim Charles II. king.

Parliament voted immediately a grant of fifty thousand pounds, a sum equal to more than two hundred thousand dollars, for the king's immediate use, with large sums besides for the other members of the family, and sent a committee of noblemen to Holland to carry the money and to invite the king back to his dominions. As soon as tidings of these events reached the Continent, every body hastened to pay their court to his majesty. From being neglected, destitute, and wretched, he suddenly found himself elevated to the highest pinnacle of prosperity and fame. Every body offered him their aid; his court was thronged, and all were ready to do him honor. The princely mother of one of the young ladies who had rejected the offer of his hand in the day of his adversity, sent him an intimation that the offer would be accepted if he would renew it now.

A fleet crossed the Channel to receive the king and convey him to London. His brother James, the Duke, of York, was placed in command of it as Lord High Admiral of England. The fleet sailed for Dover. General Monk went to Dover to receive the king at his landing. He escorted him to London, where the monarch, returning from his long exile, arrived on the twenty-ninth of May, the very day when he became thirty years of age.

General Monk, whose talent, skill, and consummate management had been the means of effecting this great change without violence or bloodshed, was rewarded by being made Duke of Albermarle. This was a very great reward. In fact, no American imagination can conceive of the images of glory and grandeur which are connected in the mind of an Englishman with the idea of being made a duke. A duke lives in a palace; he is surrounded by a court; he expends princely revenues; he reigns, in fact, often, so far as the pomp and pleasure of reigning are concerned, over quite a little kingdom, and is looked up to by the millions beneath his grade with a reverence as great, at least, as that with which the ancients looked up to their gods. He is deprived of nothing which pertains to power but the mere toil, and care, and responsibility of ruling, so that he has all the sweetness and fragrance of sovereignty without its thorns. In a word, the seat of an English duke, so far as earthly greatness and glory are concerned, is undoubtedly the finest which ambition, wealth, and power combined have ever succeeded in carving out for man. It is infinitely better than a throne.

Some historians maintain that Monk acted on a secret understanding with Charles from the commencement; that the general was to restore the king, and was then to receive a dukedom for his reward. Others say that he acted from a simple sense of duty in all that he did, and that the lofty elevation to which he was raised was a very natural and suitable testimonial of the royal gratitude. The reader will embrace the one or the other of the two theories, according to the degree of readiness or of reluctance with which he believes in the existence of conscientious principles of patriotism and loyalty among the great men who rule the world.

X

THE MARRIAGE

DURING the period of King Charles's days of adversity he made many fruitless attempts to obtain a wife. He was rejected by all the young ladies to whom he made proposals. Marriages in that grade of society are almost always mere transactions of business, being governed altogether by political and prudential considerations. In all Charles's proposals he was aiming simply at strengthening his own position by means of the wealth or family influence of the bride, supposing as he did that the honor of being even nominally a queen would be a sufficient equivalent to the lady. The ladies themselves, however, to whom he addressed himself, or their friends, thought that the prospect of his being really restored to his throne was very remote and uncertain, and, in the mean time, the empty name of queen was not worth as much as a rich and powerful heiress, by becoming his bride, would have to pay for it.

After his restoration, however, all this was changed. There was no longer any difficulty. He had now only to choose. In fact, one or two who had refused him when he was a fugitive and an exile thought differently of the case now that he was a king, and one of them, as has already been said, gave him intimations, through her friends, that if he were inclined to renew his suit, he would be more successful. Charles rejected these overtures with indignant disdain.

The lady whom he ultimately married was a Portuguese princess. Her father was King of Portugal, but before his accession to the throne his title had been the Duke of Braganza. The name of his daughter was Catharine. She is thus known generally in history by the name of Catharine of Braganza.

It is said that the plan of this marriage originated with Queen Henrietta Maria, and that a prominent motive with her in promoting the measure was her desire to secure for Charles a Catholic wife. Catharine of Braganza was a Catholic. Henrietta Maria was deeply interested, and no doubt conscientiously so, in bringing back her own family and their descendants, and the realm of England, if possible, to the ancient faith: and this question of the marriage of her son she justly considered would have a very important bearing on the result.

Queen Henrietta is said to have laid her arrangements in train for opening the negotiation with the Portuguese princess, at a visit which she made to England in 1660, very soon after her son's restoration. The Restoration took place in May. The queen's visit to her son was in October. Of course, after all the long years of danger, privation, and suffering which this family had endured, the widowed mother felt an intense emotion of joy at finding her children once more restored to what she considered their just hereditary rights. Charles was on the English throne. James, the Duke of York, was Lord High Admiral of England, that is, the commander-in-chief of the naval forces of the realm; and her other children, those who were still living, were in peace and safety. Of course, her heart was full of maternal pride and joy.

Her son James, the Lord High Admiral, went across the Channel to Dover, with a fleet of the finest ships that he could select from the whole British navy, to escort his mother to England. The queen was to embark at Calais.[7] The queen came down to the port from Paris, attended by many friends, who sympathized with her in the return of her prosperity, and were attracted, besides, by the grand spectacle which they thought would be presented by the appearance and maneuvers of the English ships, and the ceremony of the embarkation.

The waters of the English Channel are disturbed by almost perpetual agitations, which bleak winds and rapid tides, struggling continually together, combine to raise; and many a traveler, who passes in comfort across the Atlantic, is made miserable by the incessant

---

7   For a view of the famous Calais pier, see History of Mary Queen of Scots, page 105.

restlessness of this narrow sea. At the time, however, when Henrietta Maria crossed it, the waters for once were calm. The people who assembled upon the pier to witness the embarkation looked over the expanse before them, and saw it lying smooth, every where, as glass, and reflecting the great English ships which lay at a little distance from the shore as if it were a mirror. It was a bright and beautiful October morning. The air seemed perfectly motionless. The English ships were adorned with countless flags in honor of the occasion, but they all hung down perfectly lifeless upon the masts and rigging. Scarcely a ripple rolled upon the beach; and so silent and still was the morning air, that the voices and echoes came from vast distances along the shore, and the dip of the oars of the boats gliding about in the offing sent its sound for miles around over the smooth surface of the sea; and when the grand salute was fired at the embarkation of the queen, the reverberation of the guns was heard distinctly, it was said, at Dover, a distance of thirty miles.

Even in such a calm as this, however, uncommon as it is, the atmosphere is not perfectly still. When the royal party were on board the vessels and the sails were set, the fleet did begin to glide, almost imperceptibly, it is true, away from the shore. In the course of the day they had receded several miles from the land, and when the dinner hour arrived they found that the lord admiral had provided a most sumptuous banquet on board. Just before the time, however, for setting down to the table, the duke found that it was a Catholic fast day, and that neither his mother nor any of her attendants, being, as they were, all Catholics, could eat any thing but fish; and, unfortunately, as all James's men were Protestants, they had not thought of the fast, and they had no fish on board. They, however, contrived to produce a sturgeon for the queen, and they sat down to the table, the queen to the dish provided for her, and the others to bread and vegetables, and such other food as the Catholic ritual allowed, while the duke himself and his brother officers disposed, as well as they could, of the more luxurious dainties which they had intended for their guests.

With a fair wind, three hours is sufficient for the run from Calais to Dover. It took the Duke of York two days to get his fleet across in this calm. At length, however, they arrived. The king was on the pier to receive his mother. Rejoiced as her majesty must have been to be welcomed by her son under such circumstances, she must have thought mournfully of her departed husband at the time of her landing, for it was here that he had taken leave of her some years before, when the troubles of her family were beginning. Charles conducted his mother to the castle. All the inhabitants of Dover, and of the country around, had assembled to witness the arrival, and they welcomed the mother back to the land of her husband and her sons with long and loud acclamations.

There was a great banquet at Dover Castle. Here all the members of the royal family were present, having been assembled for the occasion. Of course, it was an occasion of great family rejoicing, mingled undoubtedly, on the part of the queen, with many mournful thoughts and bitter recollections. The fast was past, and there was, consequently, no difficulty now about partaking of the food that had been provided; but another difficulty arose, having the same origin, viz., the question whether the divine blessing should be implored upon the food by a Catholic priest or an Episcopal chaplain. Neither party could conscientiously acquiesce in the performance of the service by the other. They settled the important question, or rather it settled itself at last, in the following manner: When the guests were ready to take their places at table, the king, instead of asking his mother's spiritual guide to officiate, as both Christian and filial courtesy required him to have done, called upon his own chaplain. The chaplain said grace. Immediately afterward, the Catholic priest, thinking that fidelity to his own religious faith required him to act decidedly, repeated the service in the Catholic form, ending with making the sign of the cross in a very conspicuous manner over the table. The gentry of Dover, who had been admitted as spectators of this banquet, were greatly scandalized at this deed. They regarded the gesture as an act of very wicked and vary dangerous idolatry.

From Dover the queen proceeded with her children to London. Her sons did every thing in their power to honor their mother's visit; they received her with great parade and pomp, assigned her a sumptuous residence, and studied every means of amusing her, and of making her visit a source of pleasure. But they did not succeed. The queen was very unhappy. Every place that she visited recalled to her mind the memory of her husband, and awakened afresh all her sorrows. She was distressed, too, by some domestic troubles, which we have not here time to describe. Then the religious differences between herself and her children, and the questions which were arising out of them continually, gave her a great deal of pain; she could not but perceive, moreover, that she was regarded with suspicion and dislike by the people of England on account of her Catholic faith. Then, besides, notwithstanding her English husband and her English children, she was herself a French woman still in character, thought, feeling, and language, and she could not feel really at home north of the Channel. After remaining, therefore, a few months in London, and arranging some family and business affairs which required her attention, she determined to return. The king accompanied her to Portsmouth, where she set sail, taking the little princess Henrietta with her, and went back to France. Among the family affairs, however, which she arranged, it is said that the marriage of her son, the king, was a special object of her attention, and that she secretly laid the train which resulted in his espousing Catharine of Braganza.

According to the accounts given in the chronicles of the times, the negotiations were opened in the following manner: One day the Portuguese ambassador at London came to a certain high officer of the king's household, and introduced the subject of his majesty's marriage, saying, in the course of the conversation, that he thought the Princess Catharine of Portugal would be a very eligible match, and adding moreover, that he was authorized to say that, with the lady, very advantageous terms could be offered. Charles said he would think of it. This gave the ambassador sufficient encouragement to induce him to take another step. He obtained an audience of Charles the next day, and proposed the subject directly for his consideration. The ambassador knew very well that the question would turn, in Charles's mind, on the pecuniary and political advantages of the match; so he stated at once what they would be. He was authorized to offer, he said, the sum of five hundred thousand pounds[8] as the princess's portion, and to surrender to the English crown various foreign possessions, which had, till then, belonged to the Portuguese. One of the principal of these was the island of Bombay in the East Indies. Another was Tangier, a port in Africa. The English did not, at that time, hold any East Indian territories. He likewise offered to convey to the English nation the right of trading with the great South American country of Brazil, which then pertained to the Portuguese crown.

---

8 Equal to two or three millions of dollars.

Charles was very much pleased with these proposals. He immediately consulted his principal minister of state, Lord Clarendon, the celebrated historian, and soon afterward called a meeting of his privy council and laid the case before them. Clarendon asked him if he had given up all thoughts of a Protestant connection. Charles said that he did not know where to look for a Protestant wife. It was true, in fact, that nearly all the royal families of Europe were Catholics, and royal bridegrooms must always have royal brides. There were, however, Protestant princesses in Germany; this was suggested to his majesty, but he replied, with an expression of contempt, that they were all dull and foggy, and he could not possibly have one of them for a wife.

The counselors then began to look at the pecuniary and political advantages of the proposed bargain. They got out their maps, and showed Charles where Bombay, and Tangier, and the other places offered with the lady as her dowry lay. The statesmen were quite pleased with the prospect of these acquisitions, and Charles was particularly gratified with the money item. It was twice as much, they said, as any English king had ever before received as the marriage portion of a bride. In a word, the proposition was unanimously considered as in every respect entirely satisfactory, and Charles authorized his ministers to open the negotiations for the marriage immediately. All this time Charles had never seen the lady, and perhaps had never heard of her before. Her own individual qualifications, whether of mind or of person, seem to have been considered a subject not worth inquiring about at all.

Nor ought we to be at all surprised at this. It was not Charles's object, in seeking a wife, to find some one whom he was to cherish and love, and who was to promote his happiness by making him the object of her affection in return. His love, so far as such a soul is capable of love, was to be gratified by other means. He had always some female favorite, chosen from among the ladies of his court, high in rank, though not high enough to be the wedded wife of the king. These attachments were not private in any sense, nor was any attempt made to conceal them, the king being in the habit of bestowing upon the objects of them all the public attentions, as well as the private intimacy which pertain to wedded life. The king's favorite at the present time was Lady Castlemaine. She was originally a Mrs. Palmer, but the king had made her husband Lord Castlemaine for the purpose of giving a title to the wife. Some years afterward he made her a duchess. She was a prominent lady in the court, being every where received and honored as the temporary wife of the king. He did not intend, in marrying the Princess Catharine, to disturb this state of things at all. She was to be in name his wife, but he was to place his affections where he pleased. She was to have her own palace, her own household, and her own pleasures, and he, on the other hand, was to continue to have his.

Notwithstanding this, however, Charles seemed to have had some consideration for the personal appearance of his proposed bride, after all. The Spanish government, as soon as Charles's plan of espousing Catharine became known, attempted to prevent the match, as it would greatly increase the strength and influence of Portugal by giving to that country so powerful an ally. Spain had plenty of money, but no princess in the royal family; and the government therefore proposed to Charles, that if he would be content to take some Protestant lady for a wife, they would endow her, and with a portion as great as that which had been offered with Catharine. They, moreover, represented to Charles that Catharine was out of health, and very plain and repulsive in her personal appearance, and that, besides, it would be a great deal better for him, for obvious political reasons, to marry a Protestant princess. The other party replied that Catharine was not ugly by any means, and they showed Charles her portrait, which, after looking at it a few minutes, he said was *not unhandsome.* They reminded him, also, that Catharine was only the third in succession from the crown of Portugal, so that the chance of her actually inheriting that realm was not at all to be disregarded. Charles thought this a very important consideration, and, on the whole, decided that the affair should go on; and commissioners were sent to make a formal proposal of marriage at the Portuguese court. Charles wrote letters to the mother of the young lady, and to the young lady herself, expressing the personal interest he felt in obtaining the princess's hand.

The negotiations thus commenced went on for many months, with no other obstruction than the complication and intricacy which attend all matrimonial arrangements where the interests of kingdoms, as well as the personal happiness of the wedded pair, are involved in the issue. Ambassadors were sent, and contracts and treaties were drawn up, discussed, modified, and finally signed. A formal announcement of the proposed marriage was made to the English Parliament, and addresses congratulatory were voted and presented in reply. Arrangements were made for transferring the foreign possessions promised to the British crown; and, lastly, the money intended for the dower was collected, tied up in bags, sealed, and deposited safely in the strong room of the Castle at Lisbon. In fact, every thing went on prosperously to the end, and when all was thus finally settled, Charles wrote the following letter to his expected bride.

"London, 2d of July, 1661.

MY LADY AND WIFE,"
"Already the ambassador has set off for Lisbon; for me the signing of the marriage has been great happiness; and there is about to be dispatched at this time, after him, one of my servants, charged with what would appear necessary, whereby may be declared on my part the inexpressible joy of this felicitous conclusion, which, when received, will hasten the coming of your majesty."

"I am going to make a short progress into some of my provinces. In the mean time, while I am going further from my most sovereign good, yet I do not complain as to whither I go; seeking in vain tranquility in my restlessness, looking to see the beloved person of your majesty in these realms already your own; and that with the same anxiety with which, after my long banishment, I desired to see myself within them, and my subjects desiring also to behold me among them. The presence of your serenity is only wanting to unite us, under the protection of God, in the health and content I desire.

"The very faithful husband of her majesty, whose hand he kisses.
CHARLES REX."

The letter was addressed

"To the QUEEN OF GREAT BRITAIN, *my wife and lady, whom God preserve."*

Whoever reads this letter attentively will see in it that infallible criterion of hypocrisy and pretense in professions of regard, viz., extravagant ideas feebly and incoherently expressed. When the heart dictates what is said, the thoughts are natural, and the language plain; but in composition like the above, we see a continual striving to say something for effect, which the writer invents by his ingenuity as he goes on, without any honest impulses from the heart to guide him. He soars one minute and breaks down the next, in absurd alternations of the sublime and the ridiculous. How honest Charles was in such professions, and what was the kind of connubial happiness which he was preparing for his bride, is shown by the fact that he was even now spending all his time with Lady Castlemaine; and, to reconcile her to his marriage with Catharine, he had promised her that he would make her one of the ladies of the queen's bed chamber as soon as she arrived in London, which would give him constant opportunities of being in her society.

We have made very little allusion to Catharine herself, thus far, in the account of these transactions, because she has had, thus far, nothing to do with them. Every thing has been arranged for her by her mother, who was an ambitious and masculine woman, and at this time the queen regent of Portugal. Catharine had been kept shut up, all her days, in the most strict seclusion, and in the most rigorous subjection to her mother's will. It is said that she had hardly been ten times out of the palace in her life, since her return to it from the convent where she had been educated. The innocent and simple hearted maiden looked forward to her marriage as to a release from a tedious and intolerable bondage. They had shown her King Charles's picture, and had given her an account of his perilous adventures and romantic escapes, and of the courage and energy which he had sometimes displayed. And that was all she knew. She had her childlike ideas of love and of conjugal fidelity and happiness, and believed that she was going to realize them. As she looked forward, therefore, to the period of her departure for England, she longed impatiently for the time to come, her heart bounding at every thought of the happy hour with eager anticipations of delight.

An English nobleman—the Earl of Sandwich—was sent with a squadron to bring the bride to England. He was received, when he entered the Tagus, with great ceremony. A Portuguese minister went down the river to meet him in a magnificent barge. The nobleman descended to the lowest step of the ladder which led down the side of the ship, to receive the minister. They ascended the ladder together, while the ship fired a salute of twenty or thirty guns. They went into the cabin, and took seats there, with great ceremony. The minister then rose and made an address of welcome to the English commander. Lord Sandwich replied, and there was then another thundering salute of cannon.

All this parade and ceremony was, in this case, as it often is, not an *expression* of real cordiality, good will, and good faith, but a substitute for them. The English commander, who had been specially instructed to bring over the money as well as the bride, found, to his great astonishment and perplexity, that the queen regent had spent a considerable portion of the money which had been put away so safely in the bags, and she wished to pay now a part of the dowry in merchandise, at such prices as she thought reasonable, and to have a year's credit for the remainder. There was thus thrown upon Lord Sandwich the very heavy responsibility of deciding whether to give up the object of his expedition, and go back to England without the bride, or to take her without the money. After very anxious hesitation and suspense, he decided to proceed with his enterprise, and the preparations were made for the princess's embarkation.

When the day arrived, the queen descended the grand staircase of the palace, and at the foot of it took leave of her mother. Neither mother nor daughter shed a tear. The princess was conducted through the streets, accompanied by a long cavalcade and a procession of splendid carriages, through long lines of soldiers, and under triumphal arches, and over paths strewed with flowers, while bands of music, and groups of dancers, at various distances along the way, expressed the general congratulation and joy. When they reached the pier there was a splendid brigantine or barge ready to receive the bride and her attendants. The Earl of Sandwich, and other English officers of high rank belonging to the squadron, entered the barge too. The water was covered with boats, and the shipping in the river was crowded with spectators. The barge moved on to the ship which was to convey the bridal party, who ascended to the deck by means of a spacious and beautiful stair constructed upon its side. Salutes were fired by the English ships, and were echoed by the Portuguese forts on the shore. The princess's brother and the ladies who had accompanied her on board, to take leave of her there, now bade her farewell, and returned by the barge to the shore, while the ships weighed anchor and prepared to put to sea.

The wind was, however, contrary, and they were compelled to remain that night in the river; and as soon as the darkness came on, the whole shore became resplendent with illuminations at the windows in the city, and with rockets, and fire balls, and fireworks of every kind, rising from boats upon the water, and from the banks, and heights, and castle battlements all around upon the land. This gay and splendid spectacle beguiled the night, but the wind continued unfavorable all the next day, and confined the squadron still to the river. Catharine's mother sent out a messenger during the day to inquire after her daughter's health and welfare. The etiquette of royalty did not allow of her coming to see her child.

The fleet, which consisted of fourteen men-of-war, put to sea on the second day. After a long and stormy passage, the squadron arrived off the Isle of Wight; the Duke of York came out to meet it there, with five other ships, and they all entered the harbor of Portsmouth together. As soon as Catharine landed, she wrote immediately to Charles to notify him of her arrival. The news produced universal excitement in London. The bells were rung, bonfires were made in the streets, and houses were illuminated. Every body seemed full of joy and pleasure except the king himself. He seemed to care little about it. He was supping that night with Lady Castlemaine. It was five days before he set out to meet his bride, and he supped with Lady Castlemaine the night before he commenced his journey.

Some of Charles's best friends were very much grieved at his pursuing such a course; others were very indignant; but the majority of the people around him at court were like himself in character and manners, and were only led to more open irregularity and vice themselves by this public example of their sovereign. In the mean time, the king moved on to Portsmouth, escorted by a body of his Life Guards. He found that his intended bride was confined to her bed with a sort of slow fever. It was the result, they said, of the roughness and discomforts of the voyage, though we may certainly imagine another cause. Charles went immediately to the house where she was residing, and was admitted to visit her in her chamber, the many attendants who were present at the interview watching with great interest every word and look on either side by which they might judge of the nature of the first impression made by the bride and bridegroom upon each other. Catharine was not considered beautiful, and it was natural that a degree of curiosity should be manifested to learn how Charles would regard her.

There are two apparently contradictory accounts of the impression made upon Charles by this his first sight of his intended bride. Charles wrote a letter to Lord Clarendon, in which he expressed himself very well satisfied with her. He admitted that she was no beauty, but her countenance was agreeable, he said, and "her conversation," he added, "as far as I can perceive, is very good; for she has wit enough, and a very agreeable voice. You would be surprised to see how well we are acquainted already. In a word, I think myself very happy, and I am confident that we shall agree very well together. I have not time to say any more. My lord lieutenant will tell you the rest." At the same time, while writing this in his official communication to his minister, he said privately to one of his companions on leaving the presence of his bride, that, "upon his word, they had sent him a bat instead of a woman."

The royal couple were married the next day, first very privately in the Catholic form, and afterward more openly, in a great hall, and before a large assembly, according to the ritual of the Church of England. The bride was attired in the English style, her dress being of rose color, trimmed with knots of blue ribbon. These knots were, after the ceremony, detached from the dress, and distributed among the company as wedding favors, every lady eagerly pressing forward to get a share. Magnificent presents were made to the groomsmen and bridesmaids, and the company dispersed. The queen, still indisposed, went back to her bed and her supper was served to her there, the king and other members of the household partaking it with her, seated at the bedside.

A day or two afterward the royal party proceeded to London, in a long train composed of Life Guards, carriages, horsemen, baggage wagons, and attendants of every grade. The queen's heart was full of anticipations of happiness. The others, who knew what state of things she was to find on her arrival there, looked forward to scenes of trouble and woe.

XI

CHARACTER AND REIGN

SOME of the traits of character for which King Charles II. has been most noted among mankind are well illustrated by his management of the affair of Lady Castlemaine, when the queen arrived at her new home in Hampton Court. Hampton Court is a very spacious and beautiful palace on the banks of the Thames, some miles above London, splendidly built, and very pleasantly situated at a graceful bend of the river. It was magnificently fitted up and furnished for Catharine's reception. Her suite of apartments were supplied and adorned in the most sumptuous manner. Her bed, which was a present to Charles, at the time of his restoration, from the States of Holland, was said to have cost, with all the appurtenances, a sum equal to between thirty and forty thousand dollars. The hangings were an embroidery of silver on crimson velvet. The other articles of furniture in the apartment, the mirrors, the richly inlaid cabinets, the toilet service of massive gold, the canopies, the carved chairs, the curtains, the tapestries, and the paintings, corresponded in magnificence with the bed, so that Catharine, when she was introduced to the scene, felt that she had attained to the very summit of human grandeur.

For a few weeks Catharine neither saw nor heard any thing of Lady Castlemaine. She was confined to her house at the time by the care of an infant, born a few days after the arrival of the queen. Her husband had the child baptized soon after its birth as his son and heir; but the mother soon afterward had it baptized again as the son of the king, Charles himself standing sponsor on the occasion. A violent quarrel followed between Lady Castlemaine and her husband. She left the house, taking with her all her servants and attendants, and all the plate and other valuables which she could carry away. The husband, overwhelmed with wretchedness and shame, abandoned every thing, and went to France, in voluntary exile. His wife then came and took up her residence at Richmond, which is not far from Hampton Court, so as to be near the king. In all these proceedings the king himself gave her his continued countenance, encouragement, and aid.

Although Catharine, in the confiding simplicity of her character, had fully believed, in coming to London, that Charles would be to her a true and faithful husband, still she had heard the name of Lady Castlemaine before she left Lisbon. Her mother had once briefly alluded to the subject, and gave her a warning, charging her to remember the name, and to be on her guard against the lady herself, and never to tolerate her in her presence on any pretext. Things were in this state, when, one day, after Catharine had been about six weeks in her new home, Charles brought in a list of ladies whom he proposed that she should make the ladies of her household. Catharine took the list, and there, to her surprise and indignation, she saw the dreaded name of Lady Castlemaine at the head of it.

Very much agitated, she began to prick out the name, and to declare that she could not listen to any such proposition. Charles was angry, and remonstrated. She persisted, and said that he must either yield to her in that point, or send her back to Lisbon. Charles was determined to have his way, and Catharine was overwhelmed with anguish and grief. This lasted two days, when Charles made his peace with his wife by solemnly promising to give up Lady Castlemaine, and to have from that time forward nothing more to do with her.

King Charles II. has always been famed for his good nature. This was a specimen of it. He never liked to quarrel with any body, and was always ready to give up his point, in appearance and form at least, for the sake of peace and good humor. Accordingly, when he found how immovably averse his wife was to having Lady Castlemaine for an inmate of her family, instead of declaring that she must and should submit to his will, he gave up himself, and said that he would think no more about it, without, however, having the remotest idea of keeping his word. He was only intending, since he found the resistance so decided on this side of the citadel, to try to find some other approach.

Accordingly, a short time after this, one evening when the queen was holding a sort of levee in a brilliant saloon, surrounded by her Portuguese ladies, and receiving English ladies, as they were one after another presented to her by the king, the company were astonished at seeing Lady Castlemaine appear with the rest, and, as she advanced, the king presented her to the queen. To the surprise of every one, Catharine received her as graciously as the rest, and gave her her hand. The fact was, that Catharine, not being familiar with the sound and pronunciation of English words, had not understood the name. One of the Portuguese ladies who stood near her whispered to inquire if she knew that that was Lady Castlemaine. Catharine was stunned and staggered by the words as by a blow. The blood gushed from her nose, she fell over into the arms of her attendants in a fainting fit, and was borne out of the room.

There followed, after this scene, a long and dreadful quarrel. Charles accused his wife of unreasonable and foolish jealousy, and of putting a public insult upon one of the ladies of his court, whom she was bound to treat with civility and respect, since he chose to have it so. She, on the other hand, declared that he was cruel and tyrannical in making such demands upon her, and that she would go back to Portugal rather than submit to such an intolerable indignity. She criminated Charles, and Charles recriminated and threatened her, and for one night the palace was filled with the noise and uproar of the quarrel. The ladies and gentlemen of the household were very glad, they said, that they were not in London, where there would have been so many more witnesses of the scene.

Some of Charles's counselors and ministers of state were disposed at first to remonstrate with him for laying commands on his wife, with which, as they expressed it, flesh and blood could not comply. He, however, peremptorily silenced all their expostulations, and required them, as they valued his favor, to aid him in effecting his purposes. Good natured as he was, his determination was fully aroused, and he was now resolved to compel the queen to submit. He wrote a letter to Lord Clarendon, in which he declared his absolute and unalterable determination to make Lady Castlemaine "of the queen's bed chamber," and hoped he might be miserable in this world and in the world to come if he failed in the least degree in what he had undertaken; and if any one of his friends attempted to thwart or impede him in it in any way, he would make him repent of it as long as he lived. The king concluded his letter with asking Clarendon to show it to some others concerned, that they might all understand distinctly what they were to expect.

Of course, every body, after this, took sides against the queen, and all who had access to her urged her to comply with the wishes of the king. She begged and prayed to be spared such an indignity. She remonstrated, sometimes with impetuous passion, and sometimes with silent grief and bitter tears. She wanted to go back again to Portugal; but this, of course, could not be. The end of it was, that she was worn out at last. Lady Castlemaine was admitted, and remained an inmate of her family as long as she retained her place in the king's regard.

Lady Castlemaine was a proud and imperious beauty, who abused the power which she soon found that she possessed over the king, in a manner to make her an object of hatred to every one else. She interfered with every thing, and had a vast influence even over the affairs of state. The king was sometimes out of patience, and attempted resistance, but she soon reduced him to submission. There was once some question about sending a certain nobleman, who was charged with some political offenses, to the Tower. She declared that he should not be sent there. The king rebuked her interference, and they got into a high dispute on the subject, the king telling her, in the end, that she was an impertinent jade, that meddled with things she had nothing to do with. To which she replied that *he* was a great fool, that let fools have the management of his affairs, and sent his faithful servants to prison. In the end, the lady gained the victory, and the nobleman went free. Violent quarrels of this kind were very frequent between these high life lovers, and they always ended in the triumph of Lady Castlemaine. She used to threaten, as a last resort, that if the king came to an open rupture with her, she would print the letters that he had written to her, and this always brought him to terms.

These incidents indicate a very extraordinary freedom and familiarity of manners on the part of Charles, and he probably appears, in all these transactions, to much greater disadvantage in some respects than he otherwise would have done, on account of the extreme openness and frankness of his character. He lived, in fact, on the most free and familiar terms with all around him, jesting continually with every body, and taking jests, with perfect good nature, from others in return. In fact, his jests, gibes, and frolics kept the whole court continually in a condition of frivolous gayety and fun, which would have excited the astonishment of all the serious portion of mankind, if the extreme and universal dissipation and vice which prevailed had not awakened a far deeper emotion.

In fact, there seemed to be no serious element whatever in the monarch's character. He was, for instance, very fond of dogs, and cultivated a particular breed, since called King Charles's spaniels, which he kept at one time in great numbers, and in all stages of age and condition, in his palace, and in his very bed chamber, making all the apartments around very disagreeable by the effluvia. Rewards were constantly offered for certain of the king's dogs which had escaped. They were always escaping. He was attended by these dogs wherever he went, and at his meetings with his council, while the gravest and most momentous national interests were under discussion, he would amuse himself by playing with them under the table. He read his speeches at Parliament, that is, the brief messages with which the sovereign usually opens the session, in a ridiculous manner, and at church, instead of attending to the service, he would play at peep with Lady Castlemaine between the curtains which separated his box from that of the ladies of the household. And yet he pretended to be a firm believer in Christianity; and while he had no objection to any extreme of vice, he discountenanced infidelity. On one occasion, when a philosophical skeptic had been enlarging for some time on his objections to the Christian faith, Charles replied by saying, "My lord, I am a great deal older than your grace, and have heard more arguments in favor of atheism than you, but I have lived long enough to see that there is nothing in them, and I hope your grace will."

Charles spent most of his time, at some periods of his reign, in idle amusements, lounging about his palace, playing at tennis in the tennis court like a boy, and then weighing himself afterward to see how much he was gaining. In the afternoons and evenings he would loiter in the rooms of his favorites while they were finishing their dressing, gamble at cards, and often would get very much intoxicated at wild midnight carousals. He would ramble in the mall and in the parks, and feed the aquatic birds upon the ponds there, day after day, with all the interest and pleasure of a truant schoolboy. He roamed about thus in the most free and careless manner, and accosted people far beneath him in rank in what was considered a undignified way for a king.

His brother James, the Duke of York, sometimes remonstrated with him on this subject. James was, of course, so long as the queen, Charles's lawful wife, had no children, the next heir to the crown. He spent most of his life in the court of his brother, and they were generally very warm friends to each other. On one of Charles's frolicking excursions, when he was away far from his palace, without any suitable attendants or guards, James told him that he really thought his life was not safe in such exposures. Charles replied by telling James not to give himself any uneasiness. "You may depend upon it," said he, "that nobody will ever think of killing me to make *you* king."

The king was not unwilling, too, to take, himself, such jests as he gave. One day, in conversation with a dissolute member of the court, after they had been joking each other for some time, he said, "Ah! Shaftesbury, I verily believe you are the wickedest dog in my dominions."

"Yes," replied Shaftesbury, "for a *subject*, I think I am."

There was a mischievous and unmanageable goat in one of the palace courtyards, whose name was Old Rowley, and the courtiers considered the beast as affording so just an emblem of the character of the king, that they gave the king his name. Charles, instead of resenting it, entered into the jest; and one day, as he was going into the apartment of some of the ladies, be heard them singing a song, in which he figured ridiculously as the goat. He knocked at the door. They asked who was there. "Only Old Rowley," said the king.

The king's repartees were some of them really good, and he obtained in his day the reputation of being quite a wit, while yet all his actions, and the whole of his management of his affairs, were so utterly unwise and so wholly unworthy of his station, that every one was struck with the contrast. One of the wits of his court one day wrote an epitaph for him, over his door, as follows:

> *"Here lies our sovereign lord the king,*
> *Whose word no man relies on,*
> *Who never said a foolish thing,*
> *And never did a wise one."*

When the king came and saw this inscription, he stopped to read it, and said, "Yes, that is very true; and the reason is, my doings are those of my ministers, while my sayings are my own." Charles had, in fact, very little to do with the public affairs of his kingdom. He liked to build palaces and ships, and he expended vast sums, not very judiciously, on these plans. Sir Christopher Wren, the famous architect, planned one of these palaces, and Charles, when he went to see it, complained that the rooms were too small. Sir Christopher walked about with a self-important air, looking up at the ceiling, and said that he thought they were *high* enough. Sir Christopher was very small in stature. Charles accordingly squatted down as well as he could, to get his head in as low a position as the architect's, and walked about the room in that ridiculous attitude, looking up in mimicry of Sir Christopher's manner, and then said, "Oh, yes, *now* I think they are high enough."

These building plans, and other similar undertakings, together with the vast amounts which the king lavished upon his numerous female favorites, exhausted his resources, and kept him in continual straits for money. He was always urging Parliament to make new grants, and to lay more taxes, until, as he said himself, he was ashamed to look his Parliament in the face, he was so continually begging them for supplies. The people caricatured him by the representation of a poverty stricken man, with his pockets turned inside out, and begging money. At another time the caricature took the form of a man led along against his will by two women, and threatened by a third, wearing all the time a countenance expressive of helplessness and distress.

The king bore all these things with the utmost good nature, satisfied, apparently, if he could only enjoy the pleasures of dissipation and vice, and continue, in his palaces, a perpetual round of reckless merriment and fun. Some of the stories which are gravely told by the historians of the day are scarcely credible. For instance, it is said that a thief one day found his way, in the guise of a gentleman, into one of the royal drawing rooms, and contrived to get a gold snuff box out of the pocket of one of the noblemen there. Just as he had successfully accomplished his object, unobserved, as he supposed, he looked up, and saw the king's eyes fastened upon him. Knowing his majesty's character, the thief had the presence of mind to give him a wink, with a sly gesture enjoining secrecy. The king nodded assent, and the thief went away with his prize. When the nobleman missed his snuff box, the king amused himself some time with his perplexity and surprise, and then told him that it was of no use for him to search for his snuff box, for a thief had gone off with it half an hour ago. "I saw him," said the king, with a countenance full of fun, "but I could not do any thing. The rascal made me his confidant, and, of course, you know, I could not betray him."

Under the government of such a sovereign, it could not be expected that the public affairs of the realm would have gone on very prosperously. Still, however, they might have been conducted with ordinary success by his ministers, and perhaps they were, in fact, managed as well as was usual with the governments of Europe in those days. It happened, however, that three great public calamities occurred, all of a most marked and signal character, which were, perhaps, not owing at all to causes for which Charles was responsible, but which have nevertheless connected such associations in men's minds with this unfortunate reign, as that Englishmen have since looked back upon it with very little pleasure. These three calamities were the plague, the fire, and the Dutch invasion.

There have been a great many seasons of plague in London, all inconceivably dreadful; but as King Charles's fire was first among conflagrations, so his plague was the greatest pestilence that ever ravaged the city. London was, in those days, in a condition which exactly adapted it to be the easy prey of pestilence, famine, and fire. The people were crowded together in vast masses, with no comforts, no cleanliness, no proper organization. The enormous vegetable and animal accumulations of such a multitude, living more like brutes than men, produced a continual miasma, which prepared the constitutions of thousands for any infection which might chance to light among them. Pestilence is, in fact, the rude and dreadful remedy which nature provides for the human misery which man himself can not or will not cure. When the dictates of reason and conscience are neglected or disobeyed, and the ills which they might have averted sink the social state into a condition of degradation and wretchedness so great that the denser accumulations of the people become vast and corrupted swarms of vermin instead of organized communities of men, then plague and fever come in as the last resort—half remedy, half retribution—devised by that mysterious principle which struggles perpetually for the preservation of the human race, to thin off the excessive accumulation by destroying a portion of the surplus in so frightful a way as to drive away the rest in terror. The great plague of London took place in 1665, one year before the fire. The awful scenes which the whole city presented, no pen can describe. A hundred thousand persons are said to have died. The houses where cases of the plague existed were marked with a red cross and shut up, the inmates being all fastened in, to live or die, at the mercy of the infection. Every day carts rolled through the otherwise silent and desolate streets, men accompanying them to gather up with pitchforks the dead bodies which had been dragged out from the dwellings, and crying "Bring out your dead" as they went along.[9] Thousands went mad with their uncontrollable terror, and roamed about the streets in raving delirium, killing themselves, and mothers killing their children, in an insane and frenzied idea of escaping by that means, somehow or other, from the dreadful destroyer.

Every body whose reason remained to them avoided all possible contact or communication with others. Even in the country, in the exchange of commodities, a thousand contrivances were resorted to, to avoid all personal connection. In one place there was a stone, where those who had any thing to sell placed their goods and then retreated, while he who wished to buy came up, and, depositing his

---

9   Sometimes the living were pitched into the cart by mistake instead of the dead. There is a piece of sculpture in the Tottenham Court road in London intended to commemorate the following case. A Scotch piper, who had been wandering in homeless misery about the streets, with nothing but his bagpipes and his dog, got intoxicated at last, as such men always do, if they can, in times of such extreme and awful danger, and laid down upon the steps of a public building and went to sleep. The cart came along in the night, by torchlight, and one of the men who attended it, inserting the point of his fork under the poor vagabond's belt, tossed him into the cart, bagpipes and all. The dog did all he could to defend his master, but in vain. The cart went thundering on, the men walking along by its side, examining the ways for new additions to their load. The piper, half awakened by the shock of his precipitation into the cart, and aroused still more by the joltings of the road, sat up, attempted in vain to rally his bewildered faculties, looked about him, wondering where he was, and then instinctively began to play. The men, astonished and terrified at such sounds from a cart loaded with the dead, fled in all directions, leaving the cart in the middle of the street alone.
    What a mysterious and inconsistent principle is fear. Here are men braving, unconcerned and at their ease, the most absolutely appalling of all possible human dangers, and yet terrified out of their senses at an unexpected sound.

money on the stone in the place of the merchandise, took what he had thus bought away. The great fire took place in 1666, about a year after the plague, and burned a very large part of London. It commenced accidentally in a baker's shop, where a great store of fagots had been collected, and spread so rapidly among the buildings which surrounded the spot that it was soon entirely beyond control. The city of London was then composed of an immense mass of mean buildings, crowded densely together, with very narrow streets intervening, and the wind carried the flames, with inconceivable rapidity, far and wide. The people seemed struck universally with a sense of terror and despair, and nothing was to be heard but shrieks, outcries, and wild lamentations. The sky was one vast lurid canopy, like molten brass, day and night, for four days, while the whole city presented a scene of indescribable and awful din; the cracking and thundering of the flames, the frenzied screams of the women and children, the terrific falling of spires, towers, walls, and lofty battlements, the frightful explosions of the houses, blown up by gunpowder in the vain hope of stopping the progress of the flames, all formed a scene of grandeur so terrific and dreadful, that they who witnessed the spectacle were haunted by the recollection of it long afterward, as by a frightful dream. A tall monument was built upon the spot where the baker's shop stood, to commemorate the calamity. The fire held, in fact, in the estimation of mankind, the rank of the greatest and most terrible of all conflagrations, until the burning of Moscow, in the time of Napoleon, in some degree eclipsed its fame.

The Dutch invasion was the third great calamity which signalized King Charles's unfortunate reign. The ships of the enemy came up the Thames and the Medway, which is a branch of the Thames; they took possession of a fort at Sheerness, near the mouth of the river, and, after seizing all the military stores, which had been collected there to an enormous amount, they set fire to the powder magazine, and blew up the whole fortress with a terrific explosion. The way was now open to them to London, unless the English could contrive some way to arrest their progress. They attempted to do this by sinking some ships in the river, and drawing a strong chain across from one sunken vessel to the other, and fastening the ends to the shores. The Dutch, however, broke through this obstruction. They seized an opportunity when the tide was setting strongly up the river, and a fresh wind was blowing; their ships, impelled thus by a double force, broke through the chains, passed safely between the sunken ships, and came on in triumph up the river, throwing the city of London into universal consternation. There were several English ships of war, and several Dutch ships, which had been captured and brought up the Thames as prizes, lying in the river; these vessels were all seized by the Dutch, and burned; one of the English ships which they thus destroyed was called the Royal Oak.

Of course, there was now a universal scene of confusion and terror in London. Every body laid the blame of the calamity upon the king; the money which he had received for building ships, and other national defenses, he had squandered, they said, upon his guilty pleasures; then the war, which had resulted in this invasion, was caused by the political mismanagement of his reign. While the people, however, thus loudly condemned the conduct of their monarch, they went energetically at work to arrest the progress of their invaders; they sunk other ships in greater numbers, and built platforms, on which they raised batteries of cannon. At length the further progress of the enemy was stopped, and the ships were finally compelled to retire.

Among the other events which occurred during the reign of King Charles the Second, and which tended to connect unfavorable associations with the recollection of it in the minds of men, was a very extraordinary affair, which is known in history by the name of Titus Oates's Popish Plot. It was the story of a plot, said to have been formed by the Catholics, to put King Charles to death, and place his brother James, who, it will be recollected, was a Catholic, upon the throne in his stead. The story of this plot was told by a man named Titus Oates, and as it was at first generally believed, it occasioned infinite trouble and difficulty. In after times, however, the whole story came to be regarded as the fabrication of Oates, without there being any foundation for it whatever; hence the name of Titus Oates's Popish Plot, by which the affair has always since been designated in history. The circumstances were these:

Among his other various accomplishments, King Charles was quite a chemist and philosopher. He had a laboratory where he amused himself with experiments, having, of course, several persons associated with him, and attendant upon him in these researches. Among these was a man named Kirby. Mr. Kirby was an intelligent man, of agreeable manners, and of considerable scientific attainments. Charles devoted, at some periods of his life, a considerable portion of his time to these researches in experimental philosophy, and he took, likewise, an interest in facilitating the progress of others in the same pursuits. There was a small society of philosophers that was accustomed to meet sometimes in Oxford and sometimes in London. The object of this society was to provide apparatus and other facilities for making experiments, and to communicate to each other at their meetings the result of their investigations. The king took this society under his patronage, and made it, as it were, his own. He gave it the name of THE ROYAL SOCIETY, and granted it a charter, by which it was incorporated as a permanent organization, with the most ample powers. This association has since become one of the most celebrated learned societies in the world, and its establishment is one of the very few transactions of King Charles's reign which have been since remembered with pleasure.

But to return to Mr. Kirby. One day, when the king was walking in the park with a party of companions and attendants, who were separated more or less from him, as was usual on such occasions, Mr. Kirby came up to him, and, with a mysterious and earnest air, begged the king not to allow himself to be separated from the company, for his life, he said, was in danger. "Keep with your company, sir," said he, "your enemies have a design upon your life. You may be suddenly shot on this very walk." Charles was not easily frightened, and he received this announcement with great composure. He asked an explanation, however, and Mr. Kirby informed him that a plot had been formed by the Catholics to destroy him; that two men had been engaged to shoot him; and, to make the result doubly sure, another arrangement had been made to poison him. The queen's physician was the person, he said, who was charged with this latter design. Mr. Kirby said, moreover, that there was a clergyman, Dr. Tong, who was fully acquainted with all the particulars of the plot, and that, if the king would grant him an interview that evening, he would make them all known.

The king agreed to this, and in the evening Dr. Tong was introduced. He had a budget of papers which he began to open and read, but Charles had not patience to hear them; his mind was full of a plan which he was contemplating of going to Windsor the next day, to look at some new decorations which he had ordered for several of the apartments of the palace. He did not believe in the existence of any plot. It is true that plots and conspiracies were very common in those days, but false rumors and unfounded tales of plots were more common still. There was so much excitement in the minds of the community on the subject of the Catholic and Protestant faith, and such vastly extended interests depended on whether the sovereign belonged to one side or the other on this question, that every thing relating to the subject was invested with a mysterious awe, and the most wonderful stories were readily circulated and believed. The public mind was always particularly sensitive and excitable in such a case as that of Charles and his brother James at the time of which we are writing, where the reigning monarch, Charles, was of one religious faith, and his brother James, the next heir, was of the other. The death of Charles, which might at any time take place, would naturally lead to a religious revolution, and this kept the whole community in an exceedingly excitable and feverish state. There was a great temptation to form plots on the one hand, and a great eagerness to discover them on the other; and any man who could tell a story of treasonable schemes, whether his tale was true or fabricated, became immediately a personage of great importance.

Charles was well aware of these things, and was accordingly disposed to pay very little attention to Dr. Tong's papers. He said he had no time to look into them, and so he referred the whole case to the Lord Treasurer Danby, an officer of his court, whom he requested to examine into the affair. Dr. Tong, therefore, laid his papers before Danby, while the king went off the next day to Windsor to examine the new fresco paintings and the other decorations of the palace.

Danby was disposed to regard the story in a very different light from that in which it had appeared to the king. It is said that there were some charges about to be brought forward against himself for certain malpractices in his office, and that he was very much pleased, accordingly, at the prospect of having something come up to attract public attention, and turn it away from his own misdemeanors. He listened, therefore, with great interest to Dr. Tong's account of the plot, and made many minute and careful inquiries. Dr. Tong informed him that he had himself no personal knowledge of the conspiracy; that the papers, which contained all the information that he was possessed of, had been thrown into the hall of his house from the front door, and that he did not certainly know by whom, though he suspected, he said, one Titus Oates, who had formerly been a Catholic priest, and was still so far connected with the Catholics as to have very favorable opportunities to become acquainted with their designs.

Soon after this Dr. Tong had another interview with the lord treasurer, and informed him that his surmise had proved true; that it was Titus Oates who had drawn up the papers, and that he was informed in regard to all the particulars of the plot, but that he did not dare to do any thing openly in revealing them, for fear that the conspirators would kill him. The lord treasurer communicated the result of his inquiries to the king, and urged the affair upon his attention as one of the utmost possible importance. The king himself, however, was very skeptical on the subject. He laughed at the lord treasurer's earnestness and anxiety. The lord treasurer wished to have a meeting of the council called, that the case might be laid before them, but Charles refused. Nobody should know any thing about it, he said, not even his brother. It would only create excitement and alarm, and perhaps put it into somebody's head to murder him, though nobody at present had any such design.

But, notwithstanding the king's determination not to give publicity to the story of the plot, rumors of it gradually transpired, and began to excite attention. The fact that such stories were in circulation soon came to the knowledge of the Duke of York, and, of course, immediately arrested his earnest attention. As he was himself a Catholic, and the heir to the crown, any suspicion of a Catholic plot formed to dethrone his brother necessarily implicated him. He demanded an examination into the case. In a short time, vague but exaggerated rumors on the subject began to circulate through the community at large, which awakened, of course, a very general anxiety and alarm. So great was the virulence of both political and religious animosities in those days, that no one knew to what scenes of persecution or of massacre such secret conspiracies might tend Oates, whose only object was to bring himself into notice, and to obtain rewards for making known the plot which he had pretended to discover, now found, to his great satisfaction, that the fire which he had kindled was beginning to burn. The meeting of the council was called, and he was summoned to attend it. Before the time arrived, however, he went to a justice of the peace, and laid the evidence before him of the existence of the conspiracy, and of all the details respecting it which he pretended to have discovered. The name of this justice was Sir Edmondsbury Godfrey. A remarkable circumstance afterward occurred in respect to him, as will presently be related, which greatly increased and extended the popular excitement in relation to the pretended plot.

The plot, as Oates invented and detailed it, was on the most magnificent scale imaginable. The pope himself was at the head of it. The pope, he said, had laid the subject before a society of learned theologians at Rome, and they had decided that in such a case as that of England, where the sovereign and a majority of the people had renounced the true religion, and given themselves up to avowed and open heresy, the monarch lost all title to his crown, and the realms thus fallen from the faith lapsed to the pope, and were to be reclaimed by him by any mode which it seemed to him expedient to adopt. Under these circumstances, the pope had assumed the sovereignty over England, and had commissioned the society of the Jesuits—a very powerful religious society, extending over most of the countries of Europe—to take possession of the realm; that, in the prosecution of this plan, the king was to be assassinated, and that a very large sum of money had been raised and set apart, to be paid to any person who would kill the king; that an offer of ten thousand pounds had been made to the queen's physician if he would poison him. The physician had insisted upon fifteen thousand for so great a service, and this demand had finally been acceded to; and five thousand had actually been paid him in advance. Besides the murder of the king, a general assassination of the Protestants was to take place. There were twenty thousand Catholics in London, for instance, who, according to Oates's account of the plan, were to rise on a preconcerted night, and each one was to kill five Protestants, which it was thought they could easily do, as the Protestants would be taken wholly by surprise, and would be unarmed. The revolution being thus effected, the crown was to be offered to Charles's brother, the Duke of York, as a gift from the pope, and, if he should refuse to accept it on such conditions as the pope might see fit to impose, he was himself to be immediately assassinated, and some other disposal to be made of the kingdom.

Oates was examined before the council very closely, and he contradicted himself so much, and made so many misstatements about

absent persons, and the places where he pretended that certain transactions had taken place, as to prove the falseness of his whole story.
The public, however, knew little or thought little of these proofs.
They hated the Catholics, and were eager to believe and to circulate
any thing which tended to excite the public mind against them. The
most extravagant stories were accordingly circulated, and most excessive and universal fears prevailed, increasing continually by the
influence of mutual action and reaction, and of sympathy, until the
whole country was in a state of terror. A circumstance now occurred
which added tenfold to the excitement, and produced, in fact, a general consternation.

This circumstance was the sudden and mysterious death of Sir
Edmondsbury Godfrey, the justice who had taken the depositions of
Oates in respect to the conspiracy. He had been missing for several
days, and at length his body was found in a trench, by the side of a
field, in a solitary place not far from London. His own sword had
been run into his body, and was remaining in the wound. His watch
and his money were safe in his pocket, showing that he had not
been killed by robbers. This event added greatly to the excitement
that prevailed. The story was circulated that he had been killed by
the Catholics for having aided in publishing the discovery of their
plot. They who wished to believe Oates's story found in the justice's
death most ample confirmation of it. The body was brought forward
and exhibited to the public gaze in a grand procession, which moved
through the streets of London; and at the funeral guards were stationed, one on each side of the preacher, while he was delivering the
funeral discourse, to impress the people with a sense of the desperate
recklessness of Catholic hate, by the implication that even a minister
of the Gospel, in the exercise of the most solemn of his functions,
was not safe without an effectual guard.

From this time the excitement and commotion went on increasing at a very rapid rate. Oates himself, of course, became immediately a man of great importance; and to maintain himself in his new
position, he invented continually new stories, each more terrible
than the preceding. New informers, too, began to appear, confirm-
ing Oates's statements, and adding new details of their own, that
they might share his distinctions and rewards. These men became
continually more and more bold, in proportion to the increasing
readiness of the people to receive their inventions for truths. They

accused persons of higher and higher rank, until at last they dared to implicate the queen herself in their charges. They knew that, as she was a Catholic, she was unpopular with the nation at large, and as Charles had so many other lady favorites, they concluded that he would feel no interest in vindicating her from false aspersions. They accordingly brought forward accusations against the queen of having joined in the conspiracy, of having been privy to the plan of murdering the king, and of having actually arranged and directed the assassination of the justice, Sir Edmondsbury. These charges produced, of course, great excitement. The people of the country were generally predisposed to believe them true. There were various investigations of them, and long protracted examinations of the witnesses before the council and before judicial commissions appointed to inquire into and decide upon the case. These inquisitions led to debates and disputes, to criminations and recriminations without number, and they threw the whole court and the whole nation into a state of extreme excitement, some taking sides against, and some in favor of the queen. Although the popular sentiment was against her, every fair and candid mind, that attended carefully to the evidence, decided unhesitatingly in her favor. The stories of the witnesses were utterly inconsistent with each other, and in many of their details impossible. Still, so great was the public credulity, and so eager the desire to believe every thing, however absurd, which would arouse and strengthen the anti-Catholic feeling, that the queen found herself soon the object of extreme and universal odium.

The king, however, much to his credit, refused all belief of these accusations against Catharine, and strongly defended her cause. He took care to have the witnesses cross examined, and to have the inconsistencies in their testimony, and the utter impossibility that their statements could be true, pointed out. He believed, he said, that she was entirely innocent, and that the whole plan was a conspiracy to effect her destruction. "They think, I suppose," said the king, "that I should like a new wife, but I will not suffer an innocent woman to be wronged." He also told one of the ministers of state, in speaking of the subject, that, considering how hardly he had treated his wife, and how much reason she had for just complaints against him, it would be an atrocious thing for him to abandon her in such an extremity.

A volume might be filled with stories of the strange and exciting incidents that grew out of this pretended popish plot. Its consequences extended disastrously through many years, and involved a vast number of innocent persons in irretrievable ruin. The true character of Oates and his accomplices was, however, at length fully proved, and they themselves suffered the fate at last which they had brought upon others. The whole affair was a disgrace to the age. There is no circumstance connected with it which can be looked upon with any pleasure except King Charles's fidelity to his injured wife in refusing to abandon her, though he no longer loved her. His defense of her innocence, involving, as it did, a continuance of the matrimonial tie, which bound them together when all the world supposed that he wished it sundered, seems to have resulted from a conscientious sense of duty, and implies certain latent traits of generosity and nobleness in Charles's character, which, though ordinarily overpowered and nullified by the influences of folly and vice, still always seem to have maintained their hold, and to come out to view from time to time, in the course of the gay monarch's life, whenever any emergency occurred sufficient to call them into action.

The reign of King Charles the Second was signalized by many other untoward and disastrous events besides those which we have enumerated. There were unfortunate wars, great defeats in naval battles, unlucky negotiations abroad, and plots and conspiracies, dangerous and disgraceful, at home. The king, however, took all these things very good naturedly, and allowed them to interfere very little with his own personal pleasures. Whatever troubles or embarrassments affected the state, he left the anxiety and care which pertained to them to his ministers and his council, banishing all solicitude from his own mind, and enjoying himself all the time with his experiments, his ladies, his dogs, and his perpetual fun.

XII

THE CONCLUSION

TIME rolled on, and the gay and pleasure-loving king passed through one decade after another of his career, until at length he came to be over fifty years of age. His health was firm, and his mental powers vigorous. He looked forward to many years of strength and activity yet to come, and thus, though he had passed the meridian of his life, he made no preparations to change the pursuits and habits in which he had indulged himself in his early years.

He died suddenly at last, at the age of fifty-four. His death was almost as sudden as that of his father, though in a widely different way. The circumstances of his last sickness have strongly attracted the attention of mankind, on account of the manner in which the dying king was affected, at last, by remorse at the recollection of his life of reckless pleasure and sin, and of the acts to which this remorse led him upon his dying bed. The vices and crimes of monarchs, like those of other men, may be distinguished into two great types, characterized by the feelings of heart in which they take their origin. Some of these crimes arise from the malignant passions of the soul, others from the irregular and perverted action of the feelings of kindness and affection. The errors and follies of Charles, ending at last, as they did, in the most atrocious sins, were of the latter class. It was in feelings of kindness and good will toward friends of his own sex that originated that spirit of favoritism, so unworthy of a monarch, which he so often evinced; and even his irregular and unhallowed attachments of another kind seem to have been not wholly selfish and sensual. The course of conduct which he pursued through the whole course of his life toward his female companions, evinced, in many instances, a sincere attachment to them, and an honest desire to promote their welfare; and in all the wild recklessness of his life of pleasure and vice, there was seen coming out continually into view the influence of some conscientious sense of duty, and of a desire to promote the happiness of those around him, and to do justice to all. These principle were, indeed, too feeble to withstand the temptations by which they were assailed on every side; still, they did not cease to exist, and occasions were continually occurring when they succeeded in making their persuasions heard. In a word, King Charles's errors and sins, atrocious and inexcusable as they were, sprang from ill-regulated and perverted feelings of love and good will, and not from selfishness and hate; from the kindly, and not from the malignant propensities of the soul. It is very doubtful whether this is really any palliation of them, but, at any rate, mankind generally regard it so, judging very leniently, as they always do, the sins and crimes which have such an origin.

It is probable that Charles derived whatever moral principle and sensitiveness of conscience that he possessed from the influence of his mother in his early years. She was a faithful and devoted Catholic; she honestly and firmly believed that the rites and usages of the Catholic Church were divinely ordained, and that a careful and honest conformity to them was the only way to please God and to prepare for heaven. She did all in her power to bring up her children in this faith, and in the high moral and religious principles of conduct which were, in her mind, indissolubly connected with it. She derived this spirit, in her turn, from *her* mother, Mary de Medici, who was one of the most extraordinary characters of ancient or modern times. When Henrietta Maria was married to Charles I. and went to England, this Mary de Medici, her mother, wrote her a letter of counsel and of farewell, which we recommend to our readers' careful perusal. It is true, we go back to the third generation from the hero of this story to reach the document, but it illustrates so well the manner in which maternal influence passes down from age to age, and throws so much light on the strange scenes which occurred at Charles's death, and is, moreover, so intrinsically excellent, that it well merits the digression.

The queen-mother, Mary de Medici, to the young Queen of England, Henrietta Maria.

1625, June 25.

MY DAUGHTER,

You separate from me, I can not separate myself from you. I retain you in heart and memory and would that this paper could serve for an eternal memorial to you of what I am; it would then supply my place, and speak for me to you, when I can no longer speak for myself. I give you it with my last adieu in quitting you, to impress it the more on your mind, and give it to you written with my own hand, in order that it may be the more dear to you, and that it may have more authority with you in all that regards your conduct toward God, the king your husband, his subjects, your domestics, and yourself. I tell you here sincerely, as in the last hour of our converse, all I should say to you in the last hour of my existence, if you should be near me then. I consider, to my great regret, that such can never be, and that the separation now taking place between you and me for a long time, is too probably an anticipation of that which is to be forever in this world.

On this earth you have only God for a father; but, as he is eternal, you can never lose him. It is he who sustains your existence and life; it is he who has given you to a great king; it is he who, at this time, places a crown on your brow, and will establish you in England, where you ought to believe that he requires your service, and there he means to effect your salvation. Remember, my child, every day of your life, that he is your God, who has put you on earth intending you for heaven, who has created you for himself and for his glory.

The late king, your father, has already passed away; there remains no more of him but a little dust and ashes, hidden from our eyes. One of your brothers has already been taken from us even in his infancy; God withdrew him at his own good pleasure. He has retained you in the world in order to load you with his benefits; but, as he has given you the utmost felicity, it behooves you to render him the utmost gratitude. It is but just that your duties are augmented in proportion as the benefits and favors you receive are signal. Take heed of abusing them. Think well that the grandeur, goodness, and justice of God are infinite, and employ all the strength of your mind in adoring his supreme puissance, in loving his inviolable goodness; and fear his rigorous equity, which will make all responsible who are unworthy of his benefits.

Receive, my child, these instructions of my lips; begin and finish every day in your oratory,[10] with good thoughts and, in your prayers, ask resolution to conduct your life according to the laws of God, and not according to the vanities of this world, which is for all of us but a moment, in which we are suspended over eternity, which we shall pass either in the paradise of God, or in hell with the malign spirits who work evil.

Remember that you are daughter of the Church by baptism, and that this is, indeed, the first and highest rank which you have or ever will have, since it is this which will give you entrance into heaven; your other dignities, coming as they do from the earth, will not go further than the earth; but those which you derive from heaven will ascend again to their source, and carry you with them there. Render thanks to heaven each day, to God who has made you a Christian; estimate this first of benefits as it deserves, and consider all that you owe to the labors and precious blood of Jesus our Savior; it ought to be paid for by our sufferings, and even by our blood, if he requires it. Offer your soul and your life to him who has created you by his puissance, and redeemed you by his goodness and mercy. Pray to him, and pray incessantly to preserve you by the inestimable gift of his grace, and that it may please him that you sooner lose your life than renounce him. You are the descendant of St. Louis. I would recall to you, in this my last adieu, the same instruction that he received from his mother, Queen Blanche, who said to him often 'that she would rather see him die than to live so as to offend God, in whom we move, and who is the end of our being'. It was with such precepts that he commenced his holy career; it was this that rendered him worthy of employing his life and reign for the good of the faith and the exaltation of the Church. Be, after his example, firm and zealous for religion, which you have been taught, for the defense of which he, your royal and holy ancestor, exposed his life, and died faithful to him among the infidels. Never listen to, or suffer to be said in your presence, aught in contradiction to your belief in God and his only Son, your Lord and Redeemer. I entreat the Holy Virgin, whose name you bear, to deign to be the mother of your soul, and in

---

10 An oratory is a little closet furnished appropriately for prayer and other exercises of devotion.

honor of her who is mother of our Lord and Savior, I bid you adieu again and many times.

I now devote you to God forever and ever; it is what I desire for you from the very depth of my heart.

Your very good and affectionate mother,

MARIA.

From Amiens, the 10th of June, 1625.

The devout sense of responsibility to Almighty God, and the spirit of submission and obedience to his will, which this letter breathes, descended from the grandmother to the mother, and were even instilled, in some degree, into the heart of the son. They remained, however, latent and dormant through the long years of the monarch's life of frivolity and sin, but they revived and reasserted their dominion when the end came.

The dying scene opened upon the king's vision in a very abrupt and sudden manner. He had been somewhat unwell during a certain day in February, when he was about fifty-four years of age. His illness, however, did not interrupt the ordinary orgies and carousals of his palace. It was Sunday. In the evening a very gay assembly was convened in the apartments, engaged in deep gaming, and other dissolute and vicious pleasures. The king mingled in these scenes, though he complained of being unwell. His head was giddy—his appetite was gone—his walk was unsteady. When the party broke up at midnight, he went into one of the neighboring apartments, and they prepared for him some light and simple food suitable for a sick man, but he could not take it. He retired to his bed, but he passed a restless and uneasy night. He arose, however, the next morning, and attempted to dress himself, but before he finished the work he was suddenly struck by that grim and terrible messenger and coadjutor of death—apoplexy—as by a blow. Stunned by the stroke, he staggered and fell.

The dreadful paroxysm of insensibility and seeming death in a case of apoplexy is supposed to be occasioned by a pressure of blood upon the brain, and the remedy, according to the practice of those days, was to bleed the patient immediately to relieve this pressure, and to blister or cauterize the head, to excite a high external action as a means of subduing the disease within. It was the law of England that such violent remedies could not be resorted to in the case of the sovereign without authority previously obtained from the council.

They were guilty of high treason who should presume to do so. This was a case, however, which admitted of no delay. The attendants put their own lives at hazard to serve that of the king. They bled him with a penknife, and heated the iron for the cautery. The alarm was spread throughout the palace, producing universal confusion. The queen was summoned, and came as soon as possible to the scene. She found her husband sitting senseless in a chair, a basin of blood by his side, his countenance death-like and ghastly, while some of the attendants were attempting to force the locked jaws apart, that they might administer a potion, and others were applying a red hot iron to the patient's head, in a desperate endeavor to arouse and bring back again into action the benumbed and stupefied sensibilities. Queen Catharine was so shocked by the horrid spectacle that she sank down in a fit of fainting and convulsions, and was borne immediately away back to her own apartment.

In two hours the patient's suspended faculties began to return. He looked wildly about him, and asked for the queen. They sent for her. She was not able to come. She was, however, so far restored as to be able to send a message and an apology, saying that she was very glad to hear that he was better, and was much concerned that she could not come to see him; she also added, that for whatever she had done in the course of her life to displease him, she now asked his pardon, and hoped he would forgive her. The attendants communicated this message to the king. "Poor lady!" said Charles, "she beg my pardon! I am sure I beg hers, with all my heart."

Apoplexy fulfills the dread behest of its terrible master Death by dealing its blow once with a fatal energy, and then retiring from the field, leaving the stunned and senseless patient to recover in some degree from the first effect of the stroke, but only to sink down and die at last under the permanent and irretrievable injuries which almost invariably follow.

Things took this course in the case of Charles. He revived from the stupor and insensibility of the first attack, and lay afterward for several days upon his bed, wandering in mind, helpless in body, full of restlessness and pain, and yet conscious of his condition. He saw, dimly and obscurely indeed, but yet with awful certainty, that his ties to earth had been suddenly sundered, and that there only remained to him now a brief and troubled interval of mental bewilderment and bodily distress, to last for a few more hours or days, and then he must appear before that dread tribunal where his last account was to be rendered; and the vast work of preparation for the solemn judgment was yet to be made. How was this to be done? Of course, the great palace of Whitehall, where the royal patient was lying, was all in confusion. Attendants were hurrying to and fro. Councils of physicians were deliberating in solemn assemblies on the case, and ordaining prescriptions with the formality which royal etiquette required. The courtiers were thunderstruck and confounded at the prospect of the total revolution which was about to ensue, and in which all their hopes and prospects might be totally ruined. James, the Duke of York, seeing himself about to be suddenly summoned to the throne, was full of eager interest in the preliminary arrangements to secure his safe and ready accession. He was engaged night and day in selecting officers, signing documents, and stationing guards. Catharine mourned in her own sick chamber the approaching blow, which was to separate her forever from her husband, deprive her of her consequence and her rank, and consign her, for the rest of her days to the pains and sorrows, and the dreadful solitude of heart which pertains to widowhood. The king's other female intimates, too, of whom there were three still remaining in his court and in his palace, were distracted with real grief. They may have loved him sincerely; they certainly gave every indication of true affection for him in this his hour of extremity. They could not appear at his bedside except at sudden and stolen interviews, which were quickly terminated by their being required to withdraw; but they hovered near with anxious inquiries, or else mourned in their apartments with bitter grief. Without the palace the effects were scarcely less decisive. The tidings spread every where throughout the kingdom, arresting universal attention, and awakening an anxiety so widely diffused and so intense as almost to amount to a terror. A Catholic monarch was about to ascend the throne, and no one knew what national calamities were impending.

In the mean time, the dying monarch lay helpless upon his bed, in the alcove of his apartment, distressed and wretched. To look back upon the past filled him with remorse, and the dread futurity, now close at hand, was full of images of terror and dismay. He thought of his wife, and of the now utterly irreparable injuries which he had done her. He thought of his other intimates and their numerous children, and of the condition in which they would be left by his death. If he had been more entirely sensual and selfish in his attachments, he would have suffered less; but he could not dismiss these now wretched participators in his sins from his mind. He could do very little now to promote their future welfare, or to atone for the injury which he had done them; but his anxiety to do so, as well as his utter helplessness in accomplishing his desire, was evinced by his saying, in his last charge to his brother James, just before he died, that he hoped he would be kind to his children, and especially not let poor Nelly starve. [11]

Troubled and distressed with these thoughts, and still more anxious and wretched at the prospect of his own approaching summons before the bar of God, the fallen monarch lay upon his dying bed, earnestly desiring, but not daring to ask for, the only possible relief which was now left to him, the privilege of seeking refuge in the religious hopes and consolations which his mother, in years now long gone by, had vainly attempted to teach him to love. The way of salvation through the ministrations and observances of the Catholic service was the only way of salvation that he could possibly see. It is true that he had been all his life a Protestant, but Protestantism was to him only a *political* faith, it had nothing to do with moral accountability or preparation for heaven. The spiritual views of acceptance with God by simple personal penitence and faith in the atoning sacrifice of his Son, which lie at the foundation of the system of the Church of England, he never conceived of. The Church of England was to him a mere empty form; it was the service of the ancient Catholic faith, disrobed of its sanctions, despoiled of its authority, and deprived of all its spirit and soul. It was the mere idle form of godless and heartless men of the world, empty and vain. It had answered his purpose as a part of the pageantry of state during his life of pomp and pleasure, but it seemed a mockery to him now, as a means of leading his wretched and ruined soul to a reconciliation with his Maker. Every thing that was sincere, and earnest, and truly devout, in the duties of piety were associated in his mind with the memory of his mother; and as death drew nigh, he longed to return to her fold, and to have a priest, who was clothed with the authority to which her spirit had been accustomed to bow, come and be the mediator between himself and his Maker, and secure and confirm the reconciliation.

---

11   Eleanor Gwyn. She was an actress when Charles first became acquainted with her.

But how could this be done? It was worse than treason to aid or abet the tainting of the soul of an English Protestant king with the abominations of popery. The king knew this very well, and was aware that if he were to make his wishes known, whoever should assist him in attaining the object of his desire would hazard his life by the act. Knowing, too, in what abhorrence the Catholic faith was held, he naturally shrank from avowing his convictions; and thus deterred by the difficulties which surrounded him, he gave himself up to despair, and let the hours move silently on which were drawing him so rapidly toward the grave. There were, among the other attendants and courtiers who crowded around his bedside, several high dignitaries of the Church. At one time five bishops were in his chamber. They proposed repeatedly that the king should partake of the sacrament. This was a customary rite to be performed upon the dying, it being considered the symbol and seal of a final reconciliation with God and preparation for heaven. Whenever the proposal was made, the king declined or evaded it. He said he was "too weak," or "not now," or "there will be time enough yet;" and thus day after day moved on.

In the mean time, the anxious and unhappy queen had so far recovered that she came to see the king, and was often at his bedside, watching his symptoms and mourning over his approaching fate. These interviews were, however, all public, for the large apartment in which the king was lying was always full. There were ladies of the court, too, who claimed the privilege which royal etiquette accorded them of always accompanying the queen on these visits to the bedside of her dying husband. She could say nothing in private; and then, besides, her agitation and distress were so extreme, that she was incapable of any thing like calm and considerate action.

Among the favorite intimates of the king, perhaps the most prominent was the Duchess of Portsmouth. The king himself had raised her to that rank. She was a French girl, who came over, originally, from the Continent with a party of visitors from the French court. Her beauty, her wit, and her accomplishments soon made her a great favorite with the king, and for many years of his life she had exerted an unbounded and a guilty influence over him. She was a Catholic. Though not allowed to come to his bedside, she remained in her apartment overwhelmed with grief at the approaching death of her lover, and, strange as it may seem, she was earnestly desirous to obtain for him the spiritual succors which, as a Catholic, she considered essential to his dying in peace. After repeated and vain endeavors made in other ways to accomplish her object, she at length sent for the French ambassador to come to her rooms from the king's chamber, and urged him to do something to save the dying sinner's soul. "He is in heart a Catholic," said she. "I am sure he wishes to receive the Catholic sacraments. I can not do any thing, and the Duke of York is so full of business and excitement that he does not think of it. But something must be done."

The ambassador went in pursuit of the Duke of York. He took him aside, and with great caution and secrecy suggested the subject. "You are right," said the duke, "and there is no time to lose." The duke went to the king's chamber. The English clergymen had just been offering the king the sacrament once more, and he had declined it again. James asked them to retire from the alcove, as he wished to speak privately to his majesty. They did so, supposing that he wished to communicate with him on some business of state.

"Sire," said the duke to his dying brother, "you decline the sacraments of the Protestant Church, will you receive those of the Catholic?"

The countenance of the dying man evinced a faint though immediate expression of returning animation and pleasure at this suggestion. "Yes," said he, "I would give every thing in the world to see a priest."

"I will bring you one," said James.

"Do," said the king, "for God's sake, do; but shall you not expose yourself to danger by it?"

"I will bring you one, though it cost me my life," replied the duke.

This conversation was held in a whisper, to prevent its being overheard by the various groups in the room. The duke afterward said that he had to repeat his words several times to make the king comprehend them, his sense of hearing having obviously begun to fail.

There was great difficulty in procuring a priest. The French and Spanish priests about the court, who were attached to the service of the ambassadors and of the queen, excused themselves on various pretexts. They were, in fact, afraid of the consequences to themselves which might follow from an act so strictly prohibited by law. At last an English priest was found. His name was Huddleston. He had, at one time, concealed the king in his house during his adventures and wanderings after the battle of Worcester. On account of this service, he had been protected by the government of the king, ever since that time, from the pains and penalties which had driven most of the Catholic priests from the kingdom.

They sent for Father Huddleston to come to the palace. He arrived about seven o'clock in the evening. They disguised him with a wig and cassock, which was the usual dress of a clergyman of the Church of England. As the illegal ceremony about to be performed required the most absolute secrecy, it became necessary to remove all the company from the room. The duke accordingly informed them that the king wished to be alone for a short period, and he therefore requested that they would withdraw into the ante-room. When they had done so, Father Huddleston was brought in by a little door near the head of the bed, which opened directly into the alcove where the bed was laid. There was a narrow space or alley by the side of the bed, within the alcove, called the *ruelle;* [12] with this the private door communicated directly, and the party attending the priest, entering, stationed themselves there, to perform in secrecy and danger the last solemn rites of Catholic preparation for heaven. It was an extraordinary scene; the mighty monarch of a mighty realm, hiding from the vigilance of his own laws, that he might steal an opportunity to escape the consequences of having violated the laws of heaven.

They performed over the now helpless monarch the rites which the Catholic Church prescribes for the salvation of the dying sinner. These rites, though empty and unmeaning ceremonies to those who have no religious faith in them, are full of the most profound impressiveness and solemnity for those who have. The priest, having laid aside his Protestant disguise, administered the sacrament of the mass, which was, according to the Catholic views, a true and actual re-enacting of the sacrifice of Christ, to inure to the special benefit of the individual soul for which it was offered. The priest then received the penitent's confession of sin, expressed in a faint and feeble assent to the words of contrition which the Church prescribes, and this was followed by a pardon—a true and actual pardon, as the sinner supposed, granted and declared by a commissioner fully empowered by authority from heaven both to grant and declare it. Then

---

12   *Ruelle* is a French word, meaning little street or alley. This way to the bed was the one so often referred to in the histories of those times by the phrase "the back stairs".

came the "extreme unction", or, in other words, the last anointing, in which a little consecrated oil was touched to the eyelids, the lips, the ears, and the hands, as a symbol and a seal of the final purification and sanctification of the senses, which had been through life the means and instruments of sin. The extreme unction is the last rite. This being performed, the dying Catholic feels that all is well. His sins have been atoned for and forgiven, and he has himself been purified and sanctified, soul and body. The services in Charles's case occupied three quarters of an hour, and then the doors were opened and the attendants and company were admitted again.

The night passed on, and though the king's mind was relieved, he suffered much bodily agony. In the morning, when he perceived that it was light, he asked the attendants to open the curtains, that he might see the sun for the last time. It gave him but a momentary pleasure, for he was restless and in great suffering. Some pains which he endured increased so much that it was decided to bleed him. The operation relieved the suffering, but exhausted the sufferer's strength so that he soon lost the power of speech, and lay afterward helpless and almost insensible, longing for the relief which now nothing but death could bring him. This continued till about noon, when he ceased to breathe.

THE END

CPSIA information can be obtained
at www.ICGtesting.com
Printed in the USA
BVOW04s1957050617
486107BV00001B/32/P